"Do What You Do So Well That People Can't Help Telling Others About You."
— Walt Disney

to ...om Nordstrom Customer Service!

Out-Nordstrom Nordstrom

CREATING THE WORLD'S BEST CUSTOMER SERVICE

BY KEITH LEE

Fifth Edition

Foreword

If you are serious about customer service, and want your business out-perform everyone else in your industry, you need to be a serious student of the type of service that creates loyal, life-long clients. That is exactly what Keith Lee has done. And even better, he has put it down on paper so that we can all benefit from his studies.

As a business owner who supplies retailers with "everything they need to run their store," Keith has figured out that if independent retailers are not successful, he won't be successful. Therefore he has made it his professional crusade to educate and provide strategies to keep the independent retailer ahead of their competition.

Keith provided my business with our core corporate philosophy, "The Client is the Boss" (Secret Number 40), back in the 90's when he mentioned it in his newsletter. He later introduced me to *Out-Nordstrom Nordstrom Customer Service* and his *Make-You-Happy Management System* which brought together for the first time a complete and comprehensive program for insuring the type of service that has our clients raving about us.

Here is a quote from one of our clients sent to me as part of our daily email survey -

"It's heartening to see that in these days of mega-bookstores there is still a place where Customer care and service top the priority list. You instill loyalty in your Customers by providing not only excellent service and selection, but also by creating an environment that make it a pleasure to walk through the doors at Jerrol's. Thank you for consistently exceeding expectations and for being a shining example of how to run a business with class!"
Janette Paulson
Ellensburg, WA

Thanks, Keith. The norm in my industry is to go Out-of-Business. You have helped to change that for me and made my business the gold standard by which other businesses compare themselves.

Rolf T. Williams
Third generation owner
Jerrol's Book & Office Supply Co
Lots of Stuff, Fast & Fun, From People YOU Know!!
www.Jerrols.com

From the Author

While studying some of the world's best customer service companies in the early 1980's, I determined that creating an exceptional Customer Service Company was one of the best things I could do to make our company the choice for retailers. Today I am more convinced than ever that providing exceptional Customer service has been key to our success, will be key to our continued success, and can make a huge difference in the success of your business.

I recorded the Tom Peter's presentation, *In Search of Excellence* from a PBS special in the early '80s and have used it as the basis for the first day Customer service training for every team member since 1983. When the video wore out I bought a new video of the presentation, and when that wore out I bought the DVD. Today, the Disney and Stew Leonard portions of *In Search of Excellence* are included in the *Out-Nordstrom Nordstrom Customer Service System* (see the back of the book for details about this system).

While a significant amount of the information in this book is my own creation, a large amount originated with exceptional Customer service businesses like Nordstrom, Disney, FedEx, Stew Leonard's Dairy, Cabela's and others.

You might be wondering what **Out-Nordstrom Nordstrom Customer Service** means. I want you to understand that Nordstrom is a great example of exceptional Customer service and they deserve all of the Customer service accolades they've received. In fact, years ago when I received terrible Customer service from a supplier on the east coast, I told them, "Nordstrom is moving into your area; maybe you'll figure out what Customer service is all about."

The title *Out-Nordstrom Nordstrom, Creating the World's Best Customer Service* comes from Out-Nordstrom Nordstrom Customer Service Secret #53, **3 Things to Remember.** I'm a firm believer in the K.I.S.S. principle. I first heard of this from a marketing professor at the University of Puget Sound in 1978. The K.I.S.S. principle is

Keep
It
Simple
Stupid

Our '3 Things to Remember' reinforce Out-Nordstrom Nordstrom Customer Service and yet keep it simple for our team members providing the service. We use these '3 Things to Remember' in many ways - in internal communications, in initial team member training, and in ongoing training. The idea is to keep some simple ideas in front of our team members to consistently and persistently reinforce our commitment to Out-Nordstrom Nordstrom Customer Service.

One of our '3 Things to Remember' in the early 1980s was 'Out-Nordstrom Nordstrom.' Back then, and still today for many, Nordstrom is the standard for Customer service. When we decided to make exceptional Customer service our standard, our goal was to Out-Nordstrom Nordstrom. Years later, while shopping at Nordstrom and getting great Customer service, I realized that I would be disappointed if our Customers at American Retail didn't get Nordstrom quality Customer service <u>every time</u>.

I realized that we consistently Out-Nordstrom Nordstrom and our new goal should be to provide the best Customer service of any business in the world all of the time. That doesn't mean we don't fail some times.

It just means our goal is to provide the World's Best Customer Service.

This book originated as an in-house reference resource for achieving great Customer service in our company, American Retail Supply. I then shared the information in the marketing tips I send to our Customers. The response I received from the Customer service tips was so positive I decided to edit them into a resource for our Customers. From that I created this book.

If you want to receive my marketing tips go to www.AmericanRetailSupply.com and request the tips on the right side of the page.

At American Retail Supply we originally referred to Out-Nordstrom Nordstrom Customer Service as Make-You-Happy Customer Service. Make-You-Happy came from studying Walt Disney. In Tom Peter's DVD, *In Search of Excellence*, the trainer at Walt Disney World asks new cast members, "What business are we in? We know that GMC make cars, and Whirlpool makes refrigerators. What do we make here at Disney?" The answer is, **We Make People Happy...** and that's what we make at American Retail Supply. We make people happy.

You'll notice the first 37 Secrets refer to Management Philosophy Secrets and the final 22 refer to Team Member Training Secrets. You might want to read Customer Service Secret #41 first so you understand why I use the term *'Customer'* prior to secret #41 and then switch to *'Client.'*

"Remember, Only Happy Customers Come Back"

Keith Lee

The 59 Secrets

The 59 Secrets to Out-Nordstrom Nordstrom Customer Service are divided into two parts:

I. Secrets 1–37
Management philosophy, ideas, strategies, and techniques

II. Secrets 38–59
Team member training

37 Management Philosophy Secrets

1. Your core values need to put a huge emphasis on the Customer
2. The competition is anyone the Customer compares you to
3. Your Customer service expectations need to be extraordinary
4. Everyone in your company needs to know your Customer service expectations
5. Your Customers need to know your Customer service expectations
6. Your Customer service messages and actions must be consistent
7. Your Customer service messages and actions must be persistent
8. Recruit Out-Nordstrom Nordstrom team members
9. Hire people with the right attitude
10. Train for Out-Nordstrom Nordstrom Customer Service
11. Out-Nordstrom Nordstrom Customer Service should be part of your U.S.P.
12. Create symbols

13. Understand that most problems are system problems, not people problems
14. Look at errors as opportunities to retrain - don't beat people up
15. Train for exceptional 'internal' Customer service
16. Reward Customers who complain
17. Ensure that getting something done for a Customer is not dependent upon an individual
18. Ensure that your first day of training has a huge emphasis on Customer service expectations
19. Call employees 'team members'
20. Ongoing training
21. Think up-side-down
22. Put your money where your mouth is
23. Can your business pass the acid test of Out-Nordstrom Nordstrom Customer Service?
24. Be honest
25. Align yourself only with suppliers who are dedicated to the same level of Customer service that you are
26. Create systems that reinforce Out-Nordstrom Nordstrom Customer Service
27. Do your policies, procedures, and practices reinforce Out-Nordstrom Nordstrom Customer Service?
28. Have a great database
29. Are your signs positive or negative?
30. Steal and distribute good Customer service ideas
31. What business are you in?
32. Create Customer service legends
33. Managers should be seen as coaches, facilitators, and nurturers of champions - not as cops, naysayers, or devil's advocates

34. Do macro and micro well
35. Make sure all Customer service messages to Customers are also directed to team members
36. People don't work for you
37. Reward Out-Nordstrom Nordstrom Customer Service

22 Team Member Training Secrets

38. Train all team members to add <u>YOU</u> to every Customer interaction
39. Add Grandma to everything you say
40. Be sure everyone knows 'Who's The Boss'
41. Clients not Customers
42. Indifference is not an option!
43. Train all team members who come in contact with Clients in how to take care of an upset Client
44. Supervisors and managers must be able to think, act, and do
45. If someone asks to talk to a manager; give them a manager!
46. Under-promise and over-deliver
47. Ensure everyone in your company understands the 'Lifetime Value' of a Client
48. Ensure everyone in your company knows that 'Word-of-Mouth' can be your best advertising or your worst advertising
49. Challenge individuals to be Johnny
50. Train team members to understand that Clients are upset with the situation
51. SERVE THE CLIENT
52. Make sure everyone understands their role in the show
53. 3 Things to Remember
54. Ensure everyone knows your taboos

55. Use good telephone skills - Smile
56. Call people by name
57. Capitalize Client
58. Greet Clients warmly with a Smile
59. Say Thank You

Bonus Secret
All Client service problems
and errors are <u>YOUR</u> errors

The *Harvard Business Review* reports that if you can prevent 5% of your Customers from leaving, you can increase your bottom line profit by 25–95%.

A *US News and World Report* study found that the average American business loses 15% of its Customer base each year:

- 68% of Customers who stop buying from one business and go to another do so because of poor or indifferent service.
- 14% leave because of an unsatisfactorily resolved dispute or complaint.
- 9% leave because of price.
- 5% go elsewhere based on a recommendation.
- 1% die.

So 82% go somewhere else because of a Customer service issue!

With the *Harvard Business Review* reporting that you can increase your bottom line profit by 25–95% if you can prevent 5% of your Customers from leaving, and *US News and World Report* reporting that 82% of Customers leave one business and go to another because of a Customer service issue, if you are serious about staying in business, you had better be serious about Customer service.

What's sad for you and me, is that most of those Customers who leave don't bother to complain. They just leave and don't come back. Then you're stuck spending a bunch of time, money, and resources trying to get new Customers when with some consistent and persistent messages and training to both your team members and Customers, they would never have left in the first place.

It's been shown time and time again that getting new Customers is one of the most expensive things you can do to grow your business. Once we get a new Customer, we simply can't afford to lose them. **But this is great news for you!** Every business category is seeing more and more competition every year. Just about every category has a version of national chain competition, competition from discount franchises, price competition, and competition from the internet, all making it harder and harder for you to thrive. But the great news is that in this <u>most important area,</u> the reason most Customers leave one store and go to another, **you can not only beat the competition – you can crush them.**

I own four businesses, and all of them are dependent upon small independent businesses for their survival and growth. My businesses can only thrive when your business thrives, so I'm dedicated to seeing that independent small businesses not only survive, but thrive.

At our American Retail Supply 35th Anniversary Customer Appreciation Conference and EXPO, one of the speakers asked all 800 people in attendance if they had a unique product that people couldn't get anywhere else. In the entire room, only two hands went up, and I'm betting their competitors think there is a substitute product.

Almost no one has unique products or services that people can't get elsewhere, so we need to give them a reason to do business with us rather than someone else. The one area you can do that with the biggest return for your effort and money is with Out-Nordstrom Nordstrom Customer Service.

I'm not talking about Customer service in a box. This isn't about the canned, 'Thanks for shopping at Mega-Mart, have a nice day' kind of Customer service. We're talking about Out-Nordstrom Nordstrom Customer Service in which, even if you mess up, the Customer is going to come back because they like and believe in you and your staff! We're talking about the kind of Customer service in which Customers are not just satisfied, but loyal. Customer service in which Customers not only come back time and time again, but enthusiastically tell others about you.

Another great reason to give Out-Nordstrom Nordstrom Customer Service is, it's fun. People love getting Out-Nordstrom Nordstrom Customer Service. But people also love, and have a huge amount of pride, when they **give** Out-Nordstrom Nordstrom Customer Service. Out-Nordstrom Nordstrom Customer Service is fun for you! It's fun for your team! Your Customers love it! And the day goes much faster when everyone has fun.

It's fun to get notes like this one from Tanya Ashworth from Ashtan, Inc in Golden, CO: 'You get products to me quickly. You have product ready to pick up, which is really valued, and you have a staff that shows concern as well. Shelly has been a life saver twice now when I needed product at the last minute. Thank you. I think you are great and value the products, the timeliness, and especially the staff – especially Shelly!'

It's fun to read letter like this one from Cornel Rasor from Army Surplus in Sand Point, Idaho: The system has lived up to its' claims. My business has become easier to manage as well as more profitable. The support that I have received for the retail management program from Mark Turner has been superb. I wanted to let you know that I am impressed with the system and especially with the support I receive from Mark. Indeed he has become a friend in the time we have been doing business. I am always willing to be a reference for your company in the event that you need endorsement for your system and your service.

As a business owner, what's really great is that I received both of these comments and four more positive comments like them while I was on vacation.

Out-Nordstrom Nordstrom Customer Service, is not just great Customer service when you're watching, but all of the time.

Out-Nordstrom Nordstrom Customer Service Training Management Philosophy

1.

YOUR CORE VALUES NEED TO PUT A HUGE EMPHASIS ON THE CUSTOMER

The starting place for Out-Nordstrom Nordstrom Customer Service isn't exciting or fancy, but it is critical. Your core values, your vision, your mission statement, whatever is at the heart of your company, needs to put a huge emphasis on the Customer. If it doesn't, it's going to be apparent on a daily basis. Your team members simply won't believe you when you tell them that Customer service is all-important, and it's going to be reflected in the service they give your Customers.

Now don't get me wrong, I like making money as much as the next guy. In fact, the best reason to implement Out-Nordstrom Nordstrom Customer Service is to maximize your income. But if your core value is only making the most amount of money in the least amount of time, then you might as well stop reading!

I don't read our company value statement or beliefs daily, but they are the foundation of what we do at American Retail Supply. Our values are simple:

- Take care of our team members
- Take care of our Customers
- Be an honorable member of the community

You might be surprised to see that 'Take Care of Our Team Members' is listed before 'Take Care of Our Customers.' Please understand, these values aren't numbered, they are bulleted. This means that none is more important than another. And while one value isn't more important than another, they are in the order they are for a reason.

I believe if we take care of team members, they will almost automatically take care of Customers better. It is as simple as <u>what goes around comes around.</u> Team members who believe that the company has their best interests at heart will do a better job taking care of Customers.

Again, don't get me wrong. I make it perfectly clear to each new team member that when we say, 'Take care of team members,' we don't mean welfare and we don't mean baby-sitting. We mean **"providing team members with a means of helping them achieve their work and personal goals."** In some cases that means helping them find another job... and yes, we do that when what we have to offer no longer matches our team member's goals.

How do these types of core values affect the bottom line?

Ken Blanchard, author of *The One Minute Manager*, wrote an article in *Executive Excellence* and reported on a study done by the Ethics Resource Center. The Center performed an analysis of the Dow Jones for thirty years. At the time of the study, they discovered if you had invested $30,000 in the Dow for thirty years, you would have $134,000. Then they studied the twenty-one companies on the Dow that had set high ethical standards with a written published company statement that stated their purpose and function were to serve the public with high ethical standards. Had you invested your $30,000 with those twenty-one companies, with high ethical standards, you would have well over

$1,000,000. Let me ask you, which do you want, $134,000 or $1,000,000?

2.
THE COMPETITION IS ANYONE
THE CUSTOMER COMPARES YOU TO

I learned this from Disney. One of the ways people experience Disney is by telephone. Disney gets thousands of calls every day. Many of the calls are from the same people who call businesses who are known for their great telephone service. Businesses like our Customer, Cabela's, and our excellent shipping provider, FedEx.

So when the same people who call Cabela's or FedEx, or anyone with superior telephone service, call Disney, Disney understands that they are being compared to the service people get when calling Cabela's or FedEx. Disney then **does what they need to do** to "compete" with FedEx's telephone service.

So the lesson is, don't just think of your competitors as the businesses that sell the same things you do. Think of the competition as anyone who deals with your Customers in any way. Learn the best practices from anywhere you can, determine how you can use them in your business, and implement them.

Here's an example of how we did this in our business. Many years ago, we did what everyone in our industry did. When we got an order for a stock item it shipped two to four days later. I happened to call Cabela's to get some fly fishing supplies and they said the order would ship that afternoon. So, thinking of what I learned from Disney, I said to myself, "We need to do that," and we did. Today if an order is received within 30 minutes of our FedEx pick up, it ships that day.

3.
YOUR CUSTOMER SERVICE EXPECTATIONS NEED TO BE EXTRAORDINARY

When it comes to Customer service, the goal for many companies is a satisfied Customer. Sounds pretty good right? **Wrong!**

Customer Satisfaction is Worthless, Customer Loyalty is Priceless

Customer Satisfaction is Worthless, Customer Loyalty is Priceless, by Jeffrey Gitomer is one of my all time favorite business books. You can get it from us here at American Retail Supply by calling 800-427-5708, or go to www.AmercanRetailSupply.com and click on Retail Resources on the left navigation bar.

Satisfied Customers are... satisfied! If someone else has a little better price, or opens a store that's a bit more convenient, they're gone. Just think of it, if your goal is a satisfied Customer, even if you and your staff do everything perfectly, **the best you'll get is a satisfied Customer.** After all, that's the goal.

But the reality is, **if your goal is a satisfied Customer, you're often going to fall a bit short once in a while.** Then where are your Customers? Certainly, less than satisfied! So Customer satisfaction is not good enough. Your Customer service expectations need to be exceptional. You need to create not just satisfied Customers, but happy, loyal Customers.

What happens when a happy, loyal Customer finds a lower price? They're likely to stay with you or at least let you know. What happens when a competitor who's a bit more convenient moves in and your Customer is happy and loyal? They're likely to keep coming to your store.

What happens when you mess up with a happy, loyal Customer? Your happy, loyal Customer, knows that's not normal, and they're likely to tell you and let you make it right.

What happens when the subject of the products or services you offer comes up with a happy, loyal Customer? They're likely to rave about you and you're likely to get another new Customer.

Be sure that everyone in your business understands that your Customer service expectations are to create not just "satisfied" Customers but to give Customer service that creates happy, loyal Customers.

4.
EVERYONE IN YOUR COMPANY NEEDS TO KNOW YOUR CUSTOMER SERVICE EXPECTATIONS

If you want to successfully implement and deliver Out-Nordstrom Nordstrom Customer Service, you need to ensure that everyone in your business understands your Out-Nordstrom Nordstrom Customer Service Expectations.

You only have one chance to make a first impression

If you believe in Out-Nordstrom Nordstrom Customer Service it needs to be the very first training that any new employee (team member) receives.

During the first hour of employment, at American Retail Supply, every new team member receives Out-Nordstrom Nordstrom Customer Service Training. This training starts with an introduction to Out-Nordstrom Nordstrom Customer Service from the new team member's manager. The new team member then completes a workbook while watching Tom Peter's award winning DVD, *In Search of Excellence*. The new team member then continues to complete their workbook while watching the *Out-Nordstrom Nordstrom Customer Service Training* DVD. After watching both of the DVDs and completing their workbook the new team member's manager leads a discussion about Out-Nordstom Nordstrom Customer Service. We then give them this book to read before they continue with other training.

This system assures that each new team member gets the same consistent customer service training. Completing the workbook and discussing it with their manager guarantees that they actually pay attention and understand what's expected. Receiving this training during their first hour of employment reinforces that their most important responsibility is providing Out-Nordstrom Nordstrom Customer Service.

See the back of this book if you're interested in getting the exact same customer service training our team members receive at American Retail Supply.

The 5th secret to Out-Nordstrom Nordstrom Customer Service may surprise you, but it is critical.

5.
YOUR CUSTOMERS NEED TO KNOW YOUR CUSTOMER SERVICE EXPECTATIONS

American Retail Supply sells to about 10,000 clients each year and all of those clients have my direct phone number to call if we're not taking care of them. Each year I get about a half dozen phone calls from Customers who think they have not received Out-Nordstrom Nordstrom Customer Service from us. Almost all of these calls start with, 'I read in your newsletter that Customer service is important to you, and I just wanted you to know...' or 'A few months ago when I was on hold I heard that you wanted me to call if I had a problem that wasn't being taken care of...' or 'I really didn't want to bother you, but in your Marketing Tip of the Week, you said you want to be notified if I'm not happy.'

Sure, nobody likes getting calls like this but in another way I LOVE COMPLAINTS!

What's the alternative? For most businesses, the Customer doesn't want the hassle of complaining. She just doesn't care enough about you or your staff to say anything. She's the Customer who goes to the competition, and not only doesn't recommend you to others, but she may bad mouth you. Sure, I don't like getting these calls, but **I love Customers who give us the opportunity to MAKE THEM HAPPY.**

Find as many ways as you can to tell your Customers that you want to know if they are not happy

I got this idea from Stew Leonard's supermarket in Connecticut. He has a big sign with his picture that says, **'What Do You Like? What Don't You Like? I'd Like To Know.'** Every invoice we send out at American Retail Supply has a flyer that asks, 'What Do You Like? What Don't You Like? I'd Like To Know.' While it is redundant to send it out with every invoice, we do. I want to be sure that every Customer knows that they should expect Out-Nordstrom Nordstrom Customer Service and that I want to know if they don't get it.

But if you're going to ask for input from Customers, you need to act when you get it. Every Customer who writes to us or emails us at American Retail Supply, whether it's a good comment or a complaint, gets a response.

Again, every chance you have, tell your Customers you want to hear from them if they're not totally happy. Tell them when they are on hold on the telephone. Tell them with signs when they are at your place of business. Tell them in your advertising. Tell them when you communicate via email. Tell them on your web site. Tell them every way you can.

Of course, another reason you want to ask for those complaints is so you can fix the things that went wrong.

But there's another great reason. Your team members aren't likely to forget your Customer service expectations when they know that your Customers know your Customer service expectations and that you want your Customers to tell you directly when they don't get Out-Nordstrom Nordstrom Customer Service.

6.
YOUR CUSTOMER SERVICE MESSAGES
AND ACTIONS MUST BE CONSISTENT

I spent eight years working in the grocery business. I thought the company headquarters had consistent Customer service messages and expectations, but those expectations were totally undermined when, in the break room, the store manager made fun of Customers and joked about how stupid they were - even to the point of making fun of their appearance. Is it any wonder, that with a few exceptions, our Customer service was indifferent?

It's also no wonder that when a new manager came in with respect for everyone, team members and Customers alike, our Customer service level improved dramatically along with the store sales. You must never put down a Customer in front of your team members.

Be sure that your signs respect your Customers and are positive rather than negative. Rather than, 'No returns without sales receipt,' how about 'Returns gladly accepted with sales receipt.' Or 'Cash Refunds allowed with your sales receipt' instead of 'No cash refunds without sales receipt.' Or 'Checks gladly accepted with two forms of ID' instead of 'You must have two forms of ID to pay with a check.'

7.
YOUR CUSTOMER SERVICE MESSAGES AND ACTIONS MUST BE PERSISTENT

One day a newspaper reporter asked Zig Ziglar about the "motivation stuff" he was talking about. The reporter asked, "If someone attends this seminar, would they be set for life when it came to motivation?" In other words, they were asking, 'Is motivation permanent?'

Zig's reply, **'No, motivation is not permanent, but then again, neither is bathing. In fact I recommend that people bathe daily, and get a dose of motivation daily.'**

The same is true of Customer Service; I recommend and in fact, Out-Nordstrom Nordstrom Customer Service requires that you – company management – are persistent with your Customer service message.

You must find as many ways as you can to reinforce your Customer service message persistently to both your Customers and your team members. Here are a few ways we're persistent with our Customer service message:

Every contact with a Customer that comes from me ends with the sign off, 'Only Happy Customers Come Back.' Whether it's a letter, an email, the marketing tip of the week, invoice stuffers, or a message to Customers in our monthly newsletter, I always sign off with 'Remember, Only Happy Customers Come Back.'

On eight walls throughout our offices, we have a stenciled quotation from Walt Disney that says, *Do What You Do So Well That People Can't Help Telling Others About You.'* In addition, we have over thirty Disney prints throughout the office to remind people of the Disney quotation and that our job is to Make-People-Happy.

On the mirror above each sink in each bathroom, we have a small sign that says,

'The next person using this sink may be the person who makes your mortgage payment...
OUR CUSTOMER
Please show him the pride you have in serving him by leaving this restroom spotless.'

We have eight different versions of this with different colors and different sayings. For instance, a red one says, 'The next person using this sink may be the person who puts your kids through college – our Customer...' A blue one says, 'The person who will buy you your next car...'

They are in different colors so that when changed, our team members are more likely to see and read them. In addition, to ensure our team members see them, we periodically move the sign to a different spot on the mirror.

This not only reinforces our Customer service philosophy with our team members and our Customers who use our restrooms, but the restrooms are actually kept cleaner.

Here are just a few other ways to be persistent with your Out-Nordstrom Nordstrom Customer Service message:

- Your on-hold phone message
- Signage throughout your business
- In your advertising
- On your web site
- In emails

Brainstorm with your team on ways that you can reinforce your Customer service message.

8.

RECRUIT OUT-NORDSTROM NORDSTROM TEAM MEMBERS

Regardless of how you recruit, be sure that the first time a new team member candidate learns of your job and you, they see, hear, or read about your Out-Nordstrom Nordstrom Customer Service requirements.

Whether you use a newspaper ad, an employment agency, a window sign, or whatever; ensure the very first message includes a requirement to deliver exceptional Customer service.

Here are a couple of examples:

Window Sign
Hiring – Smiling Faces

Help Wanted Ad:
Retail Store Sales – 35-year-old retail business needs another great salesclerk to join fun, friendly, high performing team. Experience is good, but a GREAT CUSTOMER SERVICE ATTITUDE, drive to excel, and high energy are more important.

Another great way to get your Customer service message across and to streamline your hiring process is to have prospective candidates directed to a voicemail box where you explain the job while stressing your exceptional Customer service expectations.

9.
HIRE PEOPLE WITH THE
RIGHT ATTITUDE

You'll be delighted when you implement Out-Nordstrom Nordstrom Customer Service because hiring will be much easier. People who work where they are empowered to make Customers happy love their job. That means, when you have an opening, it will more than likely be filled by a friend or acquaintance of a current team member who has already heard of your Out-Nordstrom Nordstrom Customer Service requirements.

Over 80% of our positions at American Retail Supply are filled by referrals from our current team members... and since our team members know our Customer service expectations, they typically refer only people with an Out-Nordstrom Nordstrom attitude.

You also need to put Out-Nordstrom Nordstrom Customer Service right up front in the interview process. Be sure to include questions in the interview that will lend insight into whether this person truly believes that Out-Nordstrom Nordstrom Customer Service is part of everyone's job. Does she have a basic belief in helping others?

You might say, 'Tell me a time at your last job when you had to deal with an especially demanding Customer. How did you handle the situation?' Her answer will tell you a lot about her attitude towards Customers.

You might then ask about where she received excellent Customer service. Did she appreciate it? Did she tend to shop at that store more often?

Sure, the applicant may know the answers you want, and a particular question may not actually help in making your decision, but it will reinforce your Customer service expectations and tell the applicant right up front what is expected concerning Customer service.

So now that you've tried to find out about her basic beliefs in Customer service and you've asked specific questions concerning Customer service, before the interview is over, tell the applicant that her main job is always Customer service and that if she is hired, her first training will be in Customer service. She may be the maintenance person, the bookkeeper, a clerk, or a warehouse worker, but in your business, **EVERYONE'S PRIMARY JOB IS CUSTOMER SERVICE!**

I suggest you go to the following web site and watch the video from Grant Robinson www.HiringBestPractices.com. We have used Grant's services in our hiring for a number of years now and we do a much better job at hiring the right person for the job.

10.

TRAIN FOR OUT-NORDSTROM NORDSTROM CUSTOMER SERVICE

You can't just tell someone that you expect exceptional Customer service and get it. Out-Nordstrom Nordstrom Customer Service is not just a bunch of "rah rah" stuff and slogans.

Specific Customer Service Training is a Must

Everyone on your team needs to be trained in specific Customer interaction skills. Out-Nordstrom Nordstrom Customer Service Secrets 38 through 59 include specific Customer service training strategies that you can teach your team.

At the end of this book you'll find details about the Out-Nordstrom Nordstrom Customer Service Training System. The system includes the same first day training every new team members receives at American Retail Supply. You can use this system to train your team to implement Out-Nordstrom Nordstrom Customer Service in your business.

11.

OUT-NORDSTROM NORDSTROM CUSTOMER SERVICE SHOULD BE PART OF YOUR U.S.P.

Dan Kennedy, my favorite marketing guru, defines your Unique Selling Proposition (U.S.P.) as, **'Why should I, your prospect, do business with you verses any and every other option available to me in your category.'**

The discussion of a U.S.P. could easily take an entire book. What's important here is that in order to give

Out-Nordstrom Nordstrom Customer Service, your U.S.P. should include a focus on Customer service.

Here's our U.S.P. at American Retail Supply:
Everything you need to run your store;
on-time, every-time;
from the people who know
Only Happy Customers Come Back.'

The reference to 'Only Happy Customers Come Back' and 'on-time, every-time' are obviously Customer service driven.

What's really important about this is that each and every time you reinforce your U.S.P. with your team members or Customers you reinforce Out-Nordstrom Nordstrom Customer Service.

I have been a subscriber to Dan Kennedy's newsletter since 1992. You can learn more about Dan Kennedy and get two months of his newsletter for free at www.nobsfreegift.com/lee.

12.
CREATE SYMBOLS

I think symbols are critical for business and personal success. It is just too easy to lose track and get off course. Symbols help us stay on course and focused.

At American Retail Supply, one of the most lasting symbols that each new team member receives on their first day of employment is **'3 Things to Remember'**

- *Do What You Do So Well That People Can't Help Telling Others About You - Walt Disney*
- **...and then some**
- **What Can I Do To Make-You-Happy?**

On their first day of employment at American Retail Supply, each new employee goes through our *Out-Nordstrom Nordstrom Customer Service Training.* During that training the new team member is introduced to these '3 Things to Remember' and is told that if they come to work the next day and can tell their supervisor the '3 Things to Remember,' they'll get a $50 gift certificate to a local restaurant. This small symbol gets our Customer service message through loud and clear on the first day of employment.

Here's another example of using symbols. In eight different locations around our distribution center, we have stenciled, in eight-inch high letters:

Do What You Do So Well
That People Can't Help Telling Others About You!

Since this is a quotation from Walt Disney, we also have thirty framed prints from Disney around our distribution center as symbols to remind our team members to always deliver Out-Nordstrom Nordstrom Customer Service.

Here's another symbol. Post this sign in your lunchroom, by your time clock, in the restroom, in your backroom... wherever it makes sense for you.

**When you see, hear, or meet a Customer,
all other duties and activities are put on Hold. First,
foremost, and fanatically...
SERVE THE CUSTOMER!**

I referred to this next idea in Secret #7 and include it here to reinforce the idea that one secret can strengthen and reinforce another secret. I'm also including it again because it's simple, easy to do, and it costs you nothing. Post this little sign on the mirror in your restroom:

> The next person using this sink may be the person
> who determines the amount of your next raise...
> **Our Customer**
> Please show her the pride you have in serving her
> by leaving this restroom spotless.

Laminate and tape the sign to the mirror above the sink in your restroom (Lamination hint – Simply cover both sides with carton sealing tape and trim the edges).

With another color print:

> The next person using this sink may be the person
> who pays for your next vacation...
> **Our Customer**
> Please show her the pride you have in serving her
> by leaving this restroom spotless.

With another color:

> The next person using this sink may be the person
> who pays for your car...
> **Our Customer**
> Please show her the pride you have in serving her
> by leaving this restroom spotless.

Then every couple weeks, to get attention, change the color or move the small sign to another spot on the mirror. Your team members will see it. Your Customers will see it... and when we started using this, our restrooms were actually kept cleaner.

So again, whether you use these symbols, or make up others, I encourage you to use symbols to consistently and persistently reinforce your commitment to Out-Nordstrom Nordstrom Customer Service.

13.
UNDERSTAND THAT MOST PROBLEMS ARE SYSTEM PROBLEMS, NOT PEOPLE PROBLEMS

With the exception of a few crazy people, and I hope you don't employ any of them; nobody goes to work and says, 'How can I screw up today?' When someone screws up, or when someone does something wrong, change your thought process from blaming someone to fixing the problem permanently. When you change your thought process to changing the system rather than blaming someone, you will most often find that the problem is with the system rather than the person.

If you find yourself asking, 'Why do they always do this wrong?' **chances are they always do it wrong because it's too complicated or it's just a lot easier to do it wrong.** Make it less complicated and make it easier to do it right!

14.
LOOK AT ERRORS AS OPPORTUNITIES TO RETRAIN - DON'T BEAT PEOPLE UP

What happens when one of your team members messes up? Do they get scolded? Do they get in trouble so the next time they mess up, they want to hide their mistake?

First, you want to look at the system and see if you can improve it. Then you need to look at errors as an opportunity to retrain. When talking with co-workers and managers, consistently use the term 'retrain.'

I like to use the **"5 WHYS"** technique to find out if the problem is a system problem or a people problem. Most of the time, we find it's a system problem. There is no magic to five. It could take three "Whys" or more to get to the source of the problem.

Here's the example. Calls into accounts receivable have gone up with billing questions. So without asking five WHYS, it could be very simple to say that we need to make sure that our order entry people get it right! They must be messing up on orders.

Here's how using five WHYS can get to the heart of the problem. Customers were actually calling because they couldn't read the invoice. But why couldn't they read their invoices?

They couldn't read their invoices because the ink wasn't dark enough and it skipped once in a while. So, of course, the problem is the person who is responsible for changing the cartridge in the printer. So we yell at the guy who's supposed to change the cartridge, right? Wrong!

We ask, WHY? Why are we printing invoices that can't be read? We find that the reason we're printing unreadable invoices is that it's difficult to get the cartridges now. It never used to be difficult, but it is now because they are all kept at a central location, and we need to go there and fill out a form in order to get a cartridge. Some days we just don't have time to run up to the stock room in the middle of the day and do that. So again, we ask WHY?

Well, the facilities manager made this new procedure because he wanted more control over supplies. We go to the facilities manager and say, "Why?" His answer, 'I had to get control of supplies, because the VP of Administration came down and said we needed to reduce our supplies budget by 10%.' So it's the VP of Administration's fault right?

Let's ask him, WHY?

The answer is, the CEO looked at the financial statements and said, 'We need a 10% cut across the board on everything.' Now we finally get to the heart of the issue. It didn't have anything to do with people not trying to do their jobs as best they could. We finally found the real reason.

I encourage you, instead of looking to blame people, ask <u>WHY</u>? Get to the heart of the problem. You'll probably find it's a system problem.

But what if it's not the system and retraining isn't working. Well, not everyone works out and you may need to make changes in personnel.

15.
TRAIN FOR EXCEPTIONAL
<u>INTERNAL</u> CUSTOMER SERVICE

Ensure that all of your team members understand that yes, you have Customers, but you also have Internal Customers. Internal Customers are the people you work with. They're your vendors, your suppliers, the mailman, and of course your co-workers.

Anyone who is dependent upon
the quality of your work is your Internal Customer

Here's the idea. Our sales rep is on the phone with a Customer taking an order. Now obviously when they're on the phone taking an order, the Customer is 'the Customer.' But as they hang up the phone, "who is the customer now?" The Customer now is the person in the warehouse who's going to pull the order. If the order is not entered properly, the warehouse person can't do their job. If the rep entering the order messes up, the warehouse person will take more time than necessary, or they're not going to be able to fill the order properly. So, as soon as the sales rep hits 'process' on the order, the Customer is the warehouse person. The rep needs to make sure to take care of the Internal Customer as well as they took care of the Customer placing the order.

The warehouse person who pulls the order takes the packing list off the printer and pulls the order. Who is the Customer for the person who pulled the order?

The Customer now is the person who packages it and gets it ready to ship. If order puller doesn't pull the order properly, the guy who packages it is going to ship it wrong or he's going to hold everything up, stop, and go pull it properly.

Once the order is packaged, who is the Customer? In our case, it's the FedEx guy. If our packager hasn't packaged it properly the FedEx guy can't get it to our Customer properly and we mess up the Customer.

So this idea of Internal Customers is incredibly important. But that doesn't mean we need to be as peaches and cream when we're dealing with our Internal Customers as much as we are with external Customers? You can be yourself a little more, but you still need to give Internal Customer service that's exceptional. You still need to be what we call 'on stage' for your interaction with your Internal Customer as well.

In their training, Disney talks about 'onstage' and 'offstage.' When cast members (employees) go up into the theme park they are 'onstage' and they need to be on the top of their game. Most behind-the-scene cast member areas in Disneyland are actually under the park.

When cast members go below, away from Customers, they can be 'offstage.'

We don't agree with that at American Retail Supply. We believe that 'offstage,' away from Customers, you still need to give exceptional Internal Customer service to your teammates.

16.
REWARD CUSTOMERS WHO COMPLAIN

Don't look at complaints as problems. Look at complaints as opportunities; opportunities to improve your business and to create a better relationship with a Customer. Sure, no one really likes getting complaints, but I've learned to **love complaints!**

It's important to understand that the Customer who complains, cares enough to complain. If they didn't care, they would simply say, 'I'm not going to deal with this. I'm going somewhere else.' **I love people who complain**. They give us the opportunity to make it right for them and I can tell you without question - when you WOW a Customer with the manner in which you take care of his complaint you'll create a customer for life.

Be sure to make it perfectly clear to your Customers what they should expect. If you're reading this book you're likely doing so because you want your Customers to expect the absolute best Customer service. You need to make sure your Customers understand that's what they should expect. If they understand what is expected, and they believe you, and they like your business, they will complain and that's what you want.

You should have a system in which everything, other than major problems, is taken care of by your front line. It should be easy, quick and effortless as far as the Customer is concerned.

If it's a bigger complaint, or it comes to you specifically, you need to make sure that either you or someone with a high level of authority in your business responds to the person who complains using L.E.A.R. (see secret #43). Your biggest reward for the Customer who complains is to take care of their problem quickly and easily. WOW them with your system to take care of problems. You can also reward them with a small gift or going beyond what they would expect in taking care of the issue. An example of this comes from my friend Bill Glazer. Bill used to own menswear stores. If a Customer had a problem Bill's people were trained to fix the issue and then ask the client to pick out a free silk tie as a thank you for telling them about the problem. The ties didn't cost Bill much but they had a high perceived value from the Customer's standpoint. We tell Bill's story of silk ties when training our sales reps and teach them to offer their own silk ties to our Customers. Do you have a 'silk tie' you can use in your business?

17.
ENSURE THAT GETTING SOMETHING DONE FOR A CUSTOMER IS NOT DEPENDENT UPON AN INDIVIDUAL

Here are a couple of stories about this to show you what I mean. I needed to rent a conference room at a local hotel. I went to the closest hotel to our office and asked them about a conference room for the day. The answer was, 'Terry isn't here, and he's the only one who can help you with that.'

They couldn't even tell me whether it was booked or not. They couldn't help me in any way. How difficult would it be for Terry to leave a schedule somewhere that shows when the conference room is booked, and tell his team they can tell people if it's booked or not, but they can't actually reserve it.

So what did I do? I went to the next closest hotel. Guess what happened? The exact same thing! I was almost pulling my hair out. So I went to the next hotel. I don't know if they had the same absurd set-up or not, but I got my conference room.

Being dependent on one person to get a job done and take care of a Customer is not acceptable. If you have that going on in your business, you need to change it.

Here's another one. We love our family optometrist. He is very good and takes great care of our eyes. But sometimes his staff drives me nuts.

My wife needed to order contact lenses. She had lost hers and she wanted to get them before we went on vacation. She called the optometrist to order her contact lenses, and was told that Donna isn't in and she's the only one who orders contacts. That's absurd! Don't let your company get in this predicament.

At least make some progress. If nothing else say, 'I'll take your information right now and if there are any problems with it, we'll make sure we get back to you.' Then make sure someone can get the dang things ordered.

18.

ENSURE THAT YOUR FIRST DAY OF TRAINING HAS A HUGE EMPHASIS ON CUSTOMER SERVICE EXPECTATIONS

What's the most important asset to your company? Customers! Now let me ask you something. When you hire someone, what do you train for first? Think about it for a second. In most businesses, after the new team member fills out all of the required employment forms, what do they work on first? Maybe some product knowledge? How to ring up an order? In most businesses, it's not Customer service.

Here is an excerpt from *W.A.Y.M.I.S.H. Why Are You Making It So Hard for me to give you my money?* by Ray Considine and Ted Cohn. It does a great job of explaining what first day Customer service should be verses what it is in most organizations.

We introduce a supermarket cashier to her job by showing her how to scan, how to handle change, checks, credit cards, returns, and other necessary basic routines. We teach a new salesperson about the products, prices, terms, forms to fill out, commission, and expense routines.

Managers spend their time on the phone, writing and reading memos and reports, dealing with personnel and Customer problems, going to meetings and occasionally thinking and planning.

All of these activities are necessary. But if we are concerned with extraordinary service, we have to put them in the context of the primary purpose of every employee, at every level – to create and maintain positive Customer relationships.

Peter Drucker said it forty years ago - The purpose of BUSINESS is to create a Customer.

Start your orientation, training, and performance measurements not with activities but with Customer relationships.

With this approach of creating Customer relationships as your base, the activities fall into their proper place - as TOOLS, not ends in themselves.

Teach people to smile, be cordial, when dealing with Customers before you teach them to scan.

Teach people to listen and acknowledge feelings of others before they become product experts.

Feelings come first.

Teach people to ask questions before they give advice.

Investigate how an employee who is working on a report, straightening inventory, counting cash, or handling a personnel matter treats an encounter with a Customer. If the answer is: the Customer is interrupting the REAL work or is a distraction from the REAL job - prepare for the invasion of the WAYMISH!

And to improve the probability that your training will be used by the right people, spend a lot of time hiring people who feel comfortable with a service attitude.

You can get *W.A.Y.M.I.S.H. Why Are You Making It So Hard for me to give you my money* by calling 800-426-5708 or by visiting www.AmericanRetailSupply.com and clicking on the 'Retail Resources' link.

A great way to ensure that Customer service is a focus of the first day training for a employee is to invest in the Out-Nordstrom Nordstrom Customer Service System. You can read about this system at the end of this book.

19.
CALL EMPLOYEES TEAM MEMBERS

Frankly, I had a hard time with the whole idea of calling employees something other than employees. It seemed to be the fad to call employees "associates" or "family" or whatever. I initially thought it was just "word speak." It was all for show and really didn't mean anything. Then I heard someone refer to their employees as "team members" and I thought, "That's what

I want our business to be, a group of people working together on the common goal of providing Out-Nordstrom Nordstrom Customer Service." To me that sounded a whole lot like a team. Today we have 'team members' and not employees.

20.
ONGOING TRAINING

The best thing you can do in regards to ongoing training is all of the things you do to be consistent and persistent each day in reinforcing Out-Nordstrom Nordstrom Customer Service and practicing all of these 59 Secrets to creating Out-Nordstrom Nordstrom Customer Service.

I also suggest at least monthly <u>short</u> (10-20 minutes) Customer service training. Turn to the back of this book to learn about Done-For-You monthly managers and front line Customer service training.

In addition, at least once a year, your entire team should receive more extensive training. At American Retail Supply our entire team goes through our first day Customer service training which includes the *Out-Nordstrom Nordstrom Customer Service* DVD, the *In Search of Excellence* DVD and the workbook included in the *Out-Nordstrom Nordstrom Customer Service System*. Again, you can find out more about this system at the end of this book.

21.
THINK UP-SIDE-DOWN

Think about growing your business. What are you going to do to grow your business this year? Take a minute right now and think.

If you're like most people, when you think about growing your business, you think about getting new Customers. Mega businesses spend millions of dollars each year trying to get new Customers, and it continually amazes me that once they get me to try them, the Customer service is often so bad that I won't ever go back.

My suggestion is that when it comes to growing your business, **Think Up-Side-Down.** To grow your business, rather than thinking about getting new Customers first, **think first about keeping your existing Customers and getting them to buy more from you.**

Let's look at the numbers. Assume that 'Their Business' wants to grow by 10% this year. Let's further assume that their Customer service is typical of most businesses and two out of ten Customers decide they are going to take their business elsewhere because of lousy or indifferent Customer service. Let's assume another 5% go somewhere else for a multitude of reasons. So they lose 25% of their business each year. Now, rather than growing by 10%, 'Their Business' needs to grow by 35% to hit their target growth rate of 10%.

Now let's look at 'Your Store.' You also want to grow by 10%. But because you and everyone on your staff understands that **Customers give each of you your paycheck, and your vacations, and your raises, and everything else you get;** you simply do not lose Customers due to poor Customer service. You do lose about 5% of your Customers each year for a variety of reasons – they move, they die, misunderstandings... whatever. So for 'Your Business' after you take into account losing 5% of your Customers, you need to grow by 15% to reach your 10% growth rate.

The moral of the story is... **It's a lot easier to grow your business if you take care of your existing Customers.**

When you think about growing your business, Think Up-Side-Down. Think in this order:
1. What can I do to keep my existing Customers?
2. What can I do to increase business with my existing Customers?
and finally...
3. How can I get new Customers?

22.
PUT YOUR MONEY
WHERE YOUR MOUTH IS

Buy and distribute Customer service books and information to your team members. This does not have to be expensive. We're talking less than $50 per team member.

I recommend:

- *The Simple Truths of Service - Inspired by Johnny the Bagger,* Ken Blanchard and Barbara Glanz
- *Inside the Magic Kingdom - Seven Keys to Disney's Success,* Tom Connellan
- *W.A.Y.M.I.S.H. Why Are You Making It So Hard for me to give you my money,* Ray Considine and Ted Cohn
- *Customer Satisfaction is Worthless, Customer Loyalty is Priceless,* Jeffrey Gitomer

You can get these books at www.AmericanRetailSupply.com. Click on the 'Retail Resources' link - or call 800-426-5708. I also suggest you invest in the Out-Nordstrom Nordstrom Customer Service System. You can read about it on the last few pages of this book.

23.

CAN YOUR BUSINESS PASS THE ACID TEST OF OUT-NORDSTROM NORDSTROM CUSTOMER SERVICE?

Are the huge majority of Customer complaints resolved by the first person who talks to the Customer? See #43. Train all team members who come in contact with Customers in how to take care of an upset Customer.

If you find the majority of Customer complaints cannot be taken care of by the first person who talks to the Customer you have one of these two issues:

1. Retrain everyone on your team in Out-Nordstrom Nordstrom Customer Service Secret #43. Train all team members who come into contact with Customers in how to take care of an upset Customer.

2. If you have implemented the L.E.A.R. principle (see Secret #43) and you're still getting lots of problems that team members can't take care of, you may need to look at your basic systems and see why you're having so many problems. I strongly encourage you to examine the Make-You-Happy Management System to get your entire team on the same page and improve your business every day. For more information on the Make-You-Happy Management System go to www.KLManagementSystem.com.

24.

BE HONEST

I don't mean to be trite, but it really is true, **honesty is the best policy** - especially in dealing with your Customers.

Frankly, I can't understand how people who lie keep track of their lies. That's why most people who lie are known to be liars. They get caught. So again, honesty is the best policy in everything, but certainly in taking care of your Customers.

I've found time and time again, if you are up front and honest with your Customers when you make a mistake, they will forgive you.

Another incredibly great reason to be honest with your Customers is that you want your team members to be totally honest with you, don't you? If you're reinforcing lying by not being honest with your Customers, do you really think your team members are going to respect honesty in your business and be honest with you?

If your team members see you lying, they are much more to likely to lie to you. They will cover up things and not be honest with you and the managers in your business.

The same idea applies to family life. When my kids were two years old we paid for their airline tickets because the rule was, kids <u>under</u> two fly free. I certainly didn't want to tell my 2 year old to say he was 1 if someone asked. How could I tell him to not lie to me when I told him to lie?

25.

ALIGN YOURSELF ONLY WITH SUPPLIERS WHO ARE DEDICATED TO THE SAME LEVEL OF CUSTOMER SERVICE THAT YOU ARE

Whenever we talk to a new supplier or vendor, we tell them about our L.E.A.R. principle (Secret #43) of taking care of upset Customers. We also tell them that we expect their support to offer L.E.A.R. Customer service. If that is not the type of Customer service they plan to give to us, we won't consider them as a vendor.

In other words, if they screw up, we expect them to make it right to the extent that our Customer wants. If we screw up, the fix is on our dime. Your vendors are critical to providing Out-Nordstrom Nordstrom Customer Service. Align yourself only with honest, responsible, and ethical vendors you can rely on.

26.

CREATE SYSTEMS THAT REINFORCE OUT-NORDSTROM NORDSTROM CUSTOMER SERVICE

This is very similar to #16 – Reward Customers who complain. It's different in that you're not necessarily looking at problems here. Instead, you are trying to build a system that creates Out-Nordstrom Nordstrom Customer Service.

The best way to do this is to ask for complaints, ask for feedback, listen to your Customers, listen to your team members, and make things as smooth as possible in regards to taking care of Customers. For example, don't have a bunch of policies in your business that are negative.

For us, it's often the little things, like getting rid of five different key strokes when we're taking an order over the phone. Why do you have to press 'TAB' 'TAB' to fill in the next part of the order instead of just 'TAB' to go from one part of the order to another? With this, we save a couple seconds here and there and make taking care of clients as efficient as possible.

Look at all of your systems, listen to the people using them, watch what's going on, and design systems and procedures that make giving exceptional Customer service easy.

The best way to create systems that reinforce Out-Nordstrom Nordstrom Customer Service is to implement the Make-You-Happy Management System. With this management system, everyone on your team will be striving each day to create these types of systems.

You can find out more about the Make-You-Happy Management System at www.KLManagementSystem.com.

27.

DO YOUR POLICIES, PROCEDURES, AND PRACTICES REINFORCE OUT-NORDSTROM NORDSTROM CUSTOMER SERVICE?

Do your policies, procedures, and practices give the benefit of the doubt to your good Customers or do they punish the 99.9% of your honest and good Customers because of a very few dishonest people? Make sure your policies, practices, and procedures reinforce Out-Nordstrom Nordstrom Customer Service.

Here's an example of how the best intentions of a well-meaning team member can create a policy that punishes good Customers because of one dishonest Customer.

We sent five rolls of gift-wrap to a Customer via C.O.D. Because of the size of the rolls, each roll required a separate package, and FedEx charges for each C.O.D. tag, and we pass that charge on to the Customer. To save the Customer money, we put the entire C.O.D. fee on one package. When they were delivered the Customer accepted the four packages without the C.O.D. tags on them, and refused the one package that had the C.O.D. tag on it.

So this dishonest Customer got the four packages for free, with no intention of ever paying us. Our warehouse manager was infuriated that someone would take advantage of us, and decided that no one was going to do this again. From then on, if we had a C.O.D. that was more than one package, he would divide the amount of the total order among the packages and put that amount on each package going to the Customer That meant the Customer would pay multiple C.O.D. fees, but we would never be cheated like this again.

When I found out, I thanked the manager for doing what he thought was right to take care of us, but I explained that we don't punish our 99.9% of our honest Customers because of one dishonest Customer. In this case, it was way more than 99.9% of our Customers because we had sent out literally thousands of C.O.D. packages and this had never happened to us before. Don't punish the majority of your honest Customers because of one dishonest Customer.

Now, is this going happen to us again? Are we going to have to eat it again? Probably, but I would rather do that than charge each of our honest C.O.D. Customers more money than needed because of one dishonest Customer. (Update – FedEx has changed its policy and regardless of what we want to do, they now require us to divide the total C.O.D. fee by the number of packages).

Review at all of your policies and procedures and make sure they are not punishing the huge majority of your honest Customers because of a very few dishonest Customers.

28.

HAVE A GREAT DATABASE

I'm going to give you an idea of how important this is in our company and then I'll give you an example to see how this works for a retailer for whom I'm a Client.

We can take care of Customers quickly and much more efficiently and effectively because we've invested in our computer system, which has a great database. For instance, when you call to place your order, the history of everything you've ordered is right in front of your Customer service representative, so they can tell you exactly what you've ordered in the past. It's all right there on the screen in front of them, immediately available for both of you to make a decision.

When you call and order a custom printed product, we've set up the computer system so that all of the specifications for all of your custom products are easily available by hitting one button. That means when you re-order a custom printed product, the rep can go over all of the specs with you, while you're on the phone, and determine if anything needs to be changed or if we just process the order as before.

To process this order, all we need to do is press the button that says 'repeat.' This processes your new order the same as the original order and leads to efficiency in taking care of you, efficiency in getting the order placed as quickly as possible, and it gets your product to you at the lowest possible price.

How about in a retail environment? One of our Customers, Magnolia Hi-Fi, has a record of everything I've bought there. With that, when I go in and have a question about the stereo system I bought, they can easily look up exactly what I have and answer the question.

If they want to mail me information about a product that is complimentary to the system I have, they can go into their database, pull out everyone who has bought that product and send them the information, an update, or whatever it is to take care of us better.

You can get more information on this type of Point-of-Sale Computer System at www.POSForMyStore.com. Be sure to request the Free Retail Success kit while you're there. The kit contains:

1. **Free Book** – The 9 Questions You Must Ask Before You Invest in a POS System for Your Store
2. **Case Studies** – How 8 Independent Retailers Use Their POS Software to Grow Their Business in Any Economy
3. **Supplier Comparison Checklist** – Are you really getting what you need? Use this 123 point Comparison Checklist to compare suppliers and systems.

29.
ARE YOUR SIGNS POSITIVE OR NEGATIVE?

Signs are not passive. They are capable of delighting, as well as disappointing. **Review all of your signs and ask yourself, "Does the way this is written create a feeling of delight for the Customer?"** If the answer is 'No,' change the sign to produce the intended emotion. Minimize the use of words like 'no,' 'don't,' 'can't,' 'policy,' and 'prohibited.' Instead, tell people what they can do. Instead of 'No refunds after ten days,' how about, 'Refunds gladly accepted up to ten days after purchase.'

Rather than 'Two forms of identification are required to pay by check.' How about, 'Please share two forms of identification when paying by check. Thank you.'

30.
STEAL AND DISTRIBUTE
GOOD CUSTOMER SERVICE IDEAS

Constantly be on the lookout for Out-Nordstrom Nordstrom Customer Service ideas that you can steal from other businesses and use in your business. Now, I really don't mean steal. I mean take what you see and implement a similar system in your business.

Here's an example from our business. Years ago, it was typical for businesses in our industry to take an order one day and ship it in three or four days. We saw that businesses in other industries were shipping orders that same day they received it and changed our procedures to **Get It Done.** Today, same day shipping is standard practice for us.

Keep your eyes open on how you can improve your Customer service by "stealing" ideas from others.

31.
WHAT BUSINESS ARE YOU IN?

I used to think we were in the business of selling price guns to retail stores. Then I thought we were in the business of selling price guns and packaging to retail stores. Then I decided we were in the business of selling retailers everything they needed to operate their stores.

Now I know what business we are really in

In their first hour of employment each new team member at American Retail Supply receives *Out-Nordstrom Nordstrom Customer Service Training*. The system includes the DVD *In Search of Excellence* with a portion of Disney's new employee (guest service) training. In the DVD, the Disney trainer asks, "What business are we in? We know that GMC makes cars, and Whirlpool makes refrigerators. What do we make here at Disney?' The answer is 'We Make People Happy.' That's when it occurred to me, 'That's what we do at American Retail Supply! We make people happy." Frankly, I think that's the business every company should be in.

If you are in the business of Making People Happy, it becomes clear to every team member in your business what their job is... **Make Customers Happy.**

Now we understand that after Customers call us, they're not going to be singing 'Zippity Doo Dah,' but the reality is, our job is to make them happy, and if we don't make them happy, they won't, and they shouldn't, come back!

**Should you be in the business of
making customers happy?**

You can find out more about the *Out-Nordstrom Nordstrom Customer Service System* at the back of this book.

32.

CREATE CUSTOMER SERVICE LEGENDS

Create a culture in your business that recognizes great Customer service. One of the ways we do this is with 'Atta Boys' and 'Atta Girls.'

This is our system in which team members recognize other team members when they deliver exceptional internal or external Customer service.

Here are a few examples of recent Atta Boys and Atta Girls:

Here's an Atta Boy from Mark Turner about our POS tech crew. Remember, this gets sent to the entire company. "I asked the tech guys if they could answer a quick question (no charge) for a prospect that has RMS in one store and is adding a 2nd. Her current vendor could not, or would not, and she tried checking the web at Microsoft to no avail. Our guys agreed to help her. Brian called and left a message for the prospect and when she called back, Peter took care of her. I talked to her today. She said, 'He was wonderful! Your quote was a few hundred more than the other guys and money is tight, but you guys are getting the business for sure.'"

From Ariane in sales about Dorothy in purchasing. "Thank you Dorothy for helping me enter a Lozier order - this is my first one and Dorothy took the time to sit with me to make sure I understood how to enter the order so it made sense for sales, purchasing, and the Client! Way to go Dorothy for an 'And Then Some Attitude!'"

Should you have 'Atta Boys' and 'Atta Girls' in your business?

33.
MANAGERS SHOULD BE SEEN AS COACHES, FACILITATORS, AND NURTURERS OF CHAMPIONS - NOT AS COPS, NAYSAYERS, OR DEVIL'S ADVOCATES

If your managers are seen as cops, naysayers, devil's advocates, or slave drivers, you're going to have a really hard time implementing Out-Nordstrom Nordstrom Customer Service. To implement Out-Nordstrom Nordstrom Customer Service you need a team, and in a team, you and your managers need to be seen as coaches, facilitators, or nurturers of champions.

You need managers who want to see the business thrive through other people. An excellent resource to see how to get this done in your business is the book, *"How to Take Control of Your Life."* You can get the book for free at www.KLManagementSystem.com.

34.
DO MACRO AND MICRO WELL

Disney is an excellent example of this. When I talk about doing the macro and micro well, what I mean is doing the big things well, but also doing the little things well.

For instance, Disney does big things like, 'making a new theme park' incredibly well. The newest theme park at Disneyworld, Animal Kingdom, is an example of doing a big thing well. That's doing the macro well. But what about the micro, the small things? If you've ever been to a Disney theme park you've seen this in action.

Disney theme parks are among the cleanest places on earth. Everything is picked up - almost spotlessly 24/7. That's one example of doing the micro well. I use many Disney examples in our Customer service training at American Retail Supply so our team knew about litter at Disneyland when a number of us went to Disneyland together.

At Disneyland, a piece of litter is on the ground for about three minutes before it is picked up. One time, while we were in Los Angeles for a trade show, our team went to Disneyland. While in line for Star Tours, I saw a piece of litter way in the back behind some of the props. I told one of our sales reps, 'I bet they don't get that in three minutes.' We rode the ride and when we were done, we saw the line was gone so we went around and rode it again. As we ran through the line the second time, I saw the piece of litter was gone. That's doing the micro well!

Here's another Disney example of doing the micro well. Let's say you go to Disneyworld in the morning, park your car, and take off for the theme park. Before you even enter the theme park, you are told seven different times where you parked. They don't want you to come out at the end of the day frustrated because you can't find your car.

But what if you still forget where your car is? What happens then? You might go to a Disney employee (cast member) and say, 'I can't find my car,' or a Disney cast member will see you wandering around and ask, 'Having trouble finding your car?'

The Disney cast member will then ask if you know the approximate time you arrived that morning. He'll then look at his log and find out where they were parking people at that time. You'll find you were in 'Pluto,' aisle 'J or K' at that time. Then the cast member will run you over to that aisle and help you find your car. That's doing the micro well.

Do the big things well in your business, but don't miss the small things. Often it's the little things that WOW Customers. Can you imagine how frustrated you would be if, after a long day at Disneyland, it took you two hours to find your car; versus wandering around for ten or fifteen minutes and then someone helps you find your car in a way that would likely not happen anywhere else on earth? You would tell dozens of people about your experience.

35.
MAKE SURE ALL CUSTOMER SERVICE MESSAGES TO CUSTOMERS ARE ALSO DIRECTED TO TEAM MEMBERS

Our Marketing Tip of the Week and our newsletter often include articles and ideas on Customer service. All of the team members at American Retail Supply are required to read everything we send to Customers. They are required to know what we are telling you and what you should expect in regards to exceptional Customer service. With that, they know you heard it, they know I said it, and they know that they need to practice it. Be sure all of your Customer service messages going to Customers also go to your team members.

36.
PEOPLE DON'T WORK FOR YOU

One of my pet peeves is hearing someone say 'So and So works for me,' or 'They've worked for me for fifteen years.'

Think of it, "He works for me." It sounds almost like an owner-slave relationship. It sounds like a one-way street as far as benefits.

People should work for themselves. Now some would say that sounds selfish and doesn't lead to exceptional Customer service. If people are working for themselves, how does that jive with all of this Customer service stuff? **Perfectly!**

People come to work at your business because they can get something out of it. They don't come to work at your business because they want to do something for you. They get a paycheck. They take care of their family. They pay for school - whatever.

We're talking about a responsible relationship between the team member, the Customer, and you - as the owner. When your team member hears you say, 'I work with Bill,' you have elevated their level in your eyes, elevated their level in their eyes, and elevated the company's level in the eyes of the people who have heard you.

37.
REWARD OUT-NORDSTROM NORDSTROM CUSTOMER SERVICE

The reward can be for an individual or the team. It can be immediate or delayed. In your rewards, whether it's a free lunch, a great annual party, or whatever; **remind your team that it's your great Customer service** that allows you to stay in business and do these things.

Team Member Out-Nordstrom Nordstrom Customer Service Training

38.
TRAIN ALL TEAM MEMBERS TO ADD <u>YOU</u> TO EVERY CUSTOMER INTERACTION

This is <u>the big one</u>. If you do this right, you can screw up a lot of things and Customers will still come back to you.

People like buying from people... and people love buying from people who show that they truly care about them. I'm not sure who first coined it, but *"people like doing business with people they know, like, and trust."*

If you take nothing else out of this book, take this and implement it!

If you, and your entire team, show your Customers that you really care about them, they will be loyal Customers, not just satisfied Customers. Loyal Customers come back, even if you're a little higher priced. Loyal Customers will come back even if someone else is more convenient. Loyal Customers, and this is incredibly important, will allow you to make mistakes and they'll still come back.

You need to train people to put themselves into the sale.

Great Customer service is adding YOU to the sale

Make sure you train all of your team members to know that saying the right words is only 10% of the job when taking care of the Customer. Communication experts all agree that somewhere around 50% of person-to-person communication is based on body language. Another 40% is based on the tone and intonation, and only 10% of communication is based on what is actually said – the words! So make sure that every single person on your team understands that:
In saying the right words,
they've done only 10% of the job.

If you reinforce this daily they will automatically start putting themselves into the sale.

I was recently at a fast food outlet and the words the person said at the counter were fine, 'Thank you for coming to Betty's Fried Chicken. Can I take your order? Will that be original, extra crispy, or barbeque? What two sides would you like? You can choose from any of the two sides on the menu behind me. Thank you for your order.'

But her body language and intonation said,
'I could care less if you're here or not'

She, in fact, paid so little attention to the Customer she was serving that she started to give the change from the transaction to the wrong person.

That is **not** putting **you** into the sale. That is not what I'm talking about. That is one example of why I don't believe in scripting everything. It's hard to put yourself into the sale when everything is 100% totally scripted. Now that doesn't mean you can't give a number of scripts to your team members. But give them some leeway. Teach them the kind of greeting you want, but not necessarily the exact words to use. Teach them the kind of language you want them to say in the thank you, but not the exact way to say it. For me, I say, 'Thanks so much for your business, I really appreciate it' or 'Thanks so much for the order, I really appreciate it.' But for someone else adding the 'so much' may sound totally scripted and insincere.

Let's talk a bit more about tone and intonation. Let's look at seven words. Depending on where you put the emphasis these seven words can have five different meanings.

'I never said you stole the money.' Now what does this mean to you?

What about '**I** never said you stole the money' – Someone else said it.

'I never **said** you stole the money' – I wrote it.

'I never said **you** stole the money' – Your friend stole it.

I never said you **stole** the money' – I guess you could have considered it borrowed.

'I never said you stole the **money**' – You stole the computer.

With **intonation** alone, with seven words, you get five completely different meanings.

Again, be sure that all of your team is trained to understand that **saying the right words is only 10% of communication.** If you do that, and if your team understands that this is true, you will be 99% of the way to successfully putting YOU into the sale. And when you put YOU into the sale, Customers are loyal.

39.
ADD 'GRANDMA'
TO EVERYTHING YOU SAY

This secret is courtesy of Jeffrey Gitomer and his book, *Customer Satisfaction is Worthless, Customer Loyalty is Priceless*. If you're serious about creating world class Customer service you need to read Jeffrey's book.

Here's a sure-fire way to determine how 'what you say' will sound to the Customer before you say it, a way to 'test your talk,' so to speak.

PUT 'GRANDMA' AT THE END
OF EVERYTHINGYOU SAY.

What?

Every time you speak to a Customer, end it in your mind, with 'Grandma' – if it sounds like something you would say to your grandmother or your grandmother would want to hear, then say it. If not, don't.

How would this sound?

- *Sorry, we're closed, Grandma.*
- *Next! Grandma.*
- *What is this in reference to, Grandma?*
- *It's our policy, Grandma.*

This is the best real-world self-test I've ever found. If you wouldn't say it to your grandma, why would you say it to your Customer? Many phrases you use every day irritate Customers, and you have no clue until you insert 'Grandma' at the end.

Take five phrases you say all the time and add 'Grandma' to the end. How do they sound? Now call your grandmother and run a few by her.

You can get Jeffrey Gitomer's book, *Customer Satisfaction is Worthless, Customer Loyalty is Priceless* at www.AmericanRetailSupply.com - click on Retail Resources in the left navigation bar.

40.

BE SURE EVERYONE KNOWS
'WHO'S THE BOSS'

Be sure everyone knows where their paycheck comes from. A large corporation did a survey of their employees and asked where their paycheck came from. Eighty percent answered accounting, 10% answered the bank. After hearing about this survey, I asked our team members where their paycheck came from. I'm happy to say that, because they were trained to know the answer, 93% answered, 'Our Customers.' Be sure everyone in your company understands 'Who's The Boss.'

Who's The Boss?

There is only one boss, and whether a person shines shoes for a living or heads up the biggest corporation in the world, the boss remains the same – THE CUSTOMER.

She is the person who pays everyone's salary and who decides whether a business is going to succeed or fail. She doesn't care if a business has been around for a hundred years. The minute it starts treating her badly or taking her for granted, she'll put it out of business.

The boss, THE CUSTOMER, has bought and will buy everything you have or will have. She's bought all of your clothes, your home, your car, pays for your children's education, and your vacations. She pays all of your bills and she pays in exact proportion to the way you treat her.

The man who works inside a big office building or plant might think he works for the company that writes his paychecks, but he doesn't. He is working for the person who buys the product at the end of the line. In fact, THE CUSTOMER can fire everybody in the company from the president on down. And she can do it simply by spending her money somewhere else. Some of the largest companies that had flourishing businesses a few years ago are no longer in existence. They couldn't or didn't satisfy THE CUSTOMER. They forgot who the boss really is.

41.
CLIENTS NOT CUSTOMERS
"Client" Implies a Close Relationship in Which You Are Helping Someone (Namely... Your "Client").

This secret is courtesy of my friend Bill Glazer (BillGlazerConsulting.org). We started using this strategy at American Retail Supply in 1994. Bill was a menswear retailer when he wrote this.

Using the right term when referring to the people who patronize your store can make all the difference in the world.

With that thought in mind, STOP using the word 'Customer' and START using the word 'CLIENT.' It's a subtle change, but watch the impact it can have in the self-esteem department when you're escorting a shopper through the store.

WHY?
It's simple. The word 'Customer' implies that the person just buys things from you. But the word 'Client' implies a close relationship in which you are helping someone (namely... your 'Client').

Clients are people you care about – people with whom you have history. Customers are just people who buy from you and who may or may not ever buy from you again.

It seems that as far as common perception goes, business people tend to think of Customers as nuisances, but Clients are more important and are treated as such.

Many billion-dollar direct sales companies train their staff to refer to Customers as Clients. Go ahead. Start using the term 'Client' yourself. In fact, the entire team of sales associates should refer to Customers as Clients. Do it. And watch how much your Clients will like it and respond favorably.

An added benefit to using the term client is that each time your team member says Client rather than Customer, it reminds them that, in your business, they are expected to give extra special Out-Nordstrom Nordstrom Client Service.

So, with that in mind, in the rest of this book, I'll refer to Customers as Clients.

42.
INDIFFERENCE IS NOT AN OPTION!

You 'handle' and 'process' food with indifference - not Clients. Front-line team members need to understand that it is their job to Make Clients Happy. They need to understand that most Clients who leave one business for another do so because they were 'handled' or 'processed' with indifference.

Indifference is not an option with Out-Nordstrom Nordstrom Client Service

Sincere appreciation is the minimum level of service that is acceptable in an Out-Nordstrom Nordstrom Client service business. This needs to be made absolutely clear to every team member. You will never create loyal Clients if indifferent team members serve them.

43.
TRAIN ALL TEAM MEMBERS WHO COME IN CONTACT WITH CLIENTS HOW TO TAKE CARE OF AN UPSET CLIENT
Listen, Empathize, Ask, Resolve

We've used this L.E.A.R. system to take care of upset Clients at American Retail Supply since 1991.

I suggest you train your front-line people to implement the **L.E.A.R. System** and back it up with your new **'Make-You-Happy Guarantee'** which I'll explain later in this secret. You don't have to advertise this new guarantee when you start. Simply implement it and see how it goes. If it works, go with it. If it doesn't work for you, go back to what you have now.

P.S. I've never heard of a business implementing the Make-You-Happy Guarantee who's not kept it.

Here is the L.E.A.R. principle
L is for Listen. Listen and don't interrupt. There are many reasons we don't interrupt. We don't interrupt because, number one, it's rude. Another reason is that when you're upset, you, I, and everyone else practices what we're going to say... and we all practice it the same way, *from the beginning.* So if you interrupt, they're going to lose their place and you're going to have to listen to the whole thing all over again - from the beginning.

Then, of course, we listen to the Client because we respect the Client and know they are in fact, the boss.

E is for Empathize. Empathize means to put ourselves in their shoes. My favorite is, 'I'm sure glad you told me so I can help you.'

A is for Ask. Ask, "What can I do to Make-You-Happy?" Most of the time you don't actually have to say the words, 'What can I do to Make-You-Happy?' It's often obvious what you should do. But, sometimes you will want to actually use the words, 'What can I do to Make-You-Happy?'

The main idea though, is portraying the attitude of 'What can I do to Make-You-Happy?'

R is for Resolve. Give your team members guidelines of what they can and can't do right then and there to make the Client happy. If what the Client wants is reasonable, and it is within their guidelines, your team member needs to make the Client happy. Train them to take care of the Client right then and there.

I know, without an angry person in front of me, it's easy to explain how to implement the L.E.A.R. principle. It's a lot more difficult to implement it calmly and rationally when someone is screaming at you. You need to train your team members to understand that the Client is upset at the situation and not with them.

Train your team members to take a deep breath, and tell themselves, 'It is not me. It's the situation.' Train them to talk to themselves and make sure they are the person who stays calm and collected. Train them that there is never an excuse for getting angry or short.

If the Client is abusive, your team member needs to be trained to say, 'Sir, I'm sure I can help you.'

What if what the Client asks for is beyond your guidelines or completely unreasonable? In this case, you simply say to the Client 'I'm going to have to get a manager to see if we can do that.' Or 'Let me see if my manager can take care of that for you.' Or 'We don't have a manager here that can approve that right now, but if I can get your phone number, I'll have someone get back to you tomorrow morning, or whenever it is most convenient for you.'

In order to use the L.E.A.R. system effectively, you need to empower your front line people with your new **'Make-You-Happy Guarantee.'** I believe 'Make-You-Happy' is the best, and least costly guarantee, for almost any business.

Here's our Make-You-Happy Guarantee: 'When a Client has a problem, American Retail Supply team members are trained to ask, 'What can I do to Make-You-Happy?' In forty-three years we have never refused a Client's request to make it right.'

Does this mean we'll do anything? Just about, but my guess is that someday someone will ask for something so outrageous that we won't do it. Then we won't be able to say, 'In forty-three years we've never refused a Client's request to make it right.'

I've presented customer service seminars to dozens of different organizations and each time I ask the businesses if any have a guarantee similar to ours. In each seminar, a few people raise their hands. Then I ask them how the guarantee works. Every person, every time, answers, 'Great!'

Then I ask each of these businesses with the Make-You-Happy Guarantee, "How often do people ask for more than you would be willing to give them?" The answer is 'almost never' or 'never!'

So, if people never, or almost never, ask for more than you would be willing to give them, why would you make them jump through hoops or talk to a manager to give them what they want?

This guarantee will most likely cost you less than a guarantee in which you make an offer to the Client. More often than not, the Client will ask for much less than you would have offered. This savings will more than make up for the few times that Clients are unreasonable. You certainly will want to give your team members some guidelines. Give them a limit as to what they can do without a manager's approval.

**Then, unless the request is ridiculous,
train them to take care of the Client 'on the spot'**

But if the request is ridiculous or over their limit, train them to say, 'I'm sorry, I'm not authorized to do that, but if I can get your name and phone number, I'll be sure that our owner gives you a call tomorrow.'

So What Happens When Someone Asks For Something Really Unreasonable?

Here's what we do when someone gets really unreasonable with their request. The sales representative simply tells the Client that the owner (or sales manager) will call them. Many times the Client just needs some time to calm down. When you, as the owner or manager, gets back with them they will often have a much more reasonable request.

But what if after you call them back, their request is still not reasonable? You need to try to get them to be reasonable. But what if they simply won't be swayed?

I love advertising that, **'In forty-three years we have never refused a Client's request to make it right.'** With this, we have taken care of some very unreasonable requests. But again, they are few and far between.

If the unreasonable request is ridiculous and expensive, we do what the Client wants and then we code their account to say, "Client has requested unreasonable Make-You-Happy Guarantee." This alerts us so that if the Client makes an unreasonable request a second time, we do what they want again, and then after the second unreasonable request, we code the account not to sell to them in the future.

In Forty-Three Years, We Have Sold To Over 100,000 Clients And We Have Coded Only Two Accounts To Not Do Business With In The Future!

There are a number of reasons for using Make-You-Happy as your guarantee and L.E.A.R. as your system to take care of upset Clients.

- It's easy for you, your team members, and your Clients. Neither you, nor your team members, needs to play Solomon and come up with what is 'fair.'
- It's easy to train your employees.
- It costs less. Everyone I know who uses this agrees – It Costs Less.
- **It creates happy Clients – and 'Only Happy Clients Come Back!'** In addition, happy Clients spread positive word-of-mouth advertising and unhappy Clients spread negative word-of-mouth advertising.
- It makes your job easier and less hectic.

Type this up, laminate it, and have every member of your team keep it close by:

Listen - and don't interrupt.

Empathize - with something like, 'I'm sure glad you told me so I can help you.'

Ask - "What can I do to Make-You-Happy?"

Resolve - Unless what the Client asks for is ridiculous, DO IT!

44.
SUPERVISORS AND MANAGERS MUST BE ABLE TO THINK, ACT, AND DO

The L.E.A.R. principle and your Make-You-Happy Guarantee might say that in your business, a front line person is able to take care of a Client for anything up to $20. A manager might then be able to take care of any problem a Client might have up to $200 without getting you involved. That's giving managers and supervisors the ability to get things done. The ability to think, act, and do, and take care of Clients.

The Make-You-Happy Guarantee says, "If we ever let you down, we'll ask, 'What can I do to make you happy?' In forty-three years of business we've never refused a Client's request to make it right."

Sometimes, I'm on vacation and can't be contacted. I tend to go to places where there are no cell phones. What happens in that instance? What happens if someone asks for something truly crazy while I'm not there and they demand a solution right now? I've given my managers a lot of leeway. They are to use their best judgment and do what's right, and since they've seen what we've done in the past and we've discussed it, I'm confident in their judgment.

So if the Client's request is crazy and has to be taken care of before I get back, my top managers are instructed to make a decision as to whether to do it or not, and whatever their decision is, I'll accept it. They know I'll be disappointed if we need to say 'no' to a Client and I can no longer use my Make-You-Happy Guarantee as it is, but I'll be happy they made a decision and I'll trust their judgment.

45.
IF SOMEONE ASKS TO TALK TO A MANAGER; GIVE THEM A MANAGER!

Sure, you may need to ask a couple questions to get them to the proper manager, but make sure that's the only reason you are asking. When someone asks to talk to a manager, give them a manager. If one is not around, give them the person who is in charge to help them as best they can.

46.
UNDER-PROMISE AND OVER-DELIVER

Again, this is something Disney does well. If you're in line for a ride at Disneyland, and see a sign that says, "The wait from this point is 35 minutes." The actual wait will in less than thirty-five minutes. That's under-promise and over-deliver.

This principle applies to many areas. Here are some examples. If you tell a Client that someone will get back to them within a certain amount of time, you need to make sure they are gotten back to before that time.

In our business, we sell a lot of custom printed items. If we think the item is going to take three weeks to get, we'll quote four weeks. Then when the Client gets the product in three weeks, we're a hero, instead of a goat when we say three weeks, and something goes wrong. We would rather err on the side of under-promising and over-delivering.

Now that doesn't mean that we're going to walk away from orders that are tight. For example, a Client has a trade show coming up, and they need their custom printed bags before the trade show. After the trade show, those bags aren't worth anything to them. We know it's going to be a tight deadline. First, we make sure the Client knows that the bags will only be on time if everything goes well. Then we'll make phone calls or whatever needs to be done to ensure that we can make that deadline. The key is that we need to follow up on that order every single step along the line to make sure we make the deadline.

Here's another example. We may have a supplier who's providing us a product and we don't know exactly when we're going to get it. In that case, we need to allow the Client to make the decision as to whether they want it or not. We may say something like, 'If everything goes right we expect that container to be here by then, but we don't have any control if US Customs decides to delay it by inspecting it, so I just want to be sure you understand.' Again, this goes back to the idea of being totally honest with your Client. **Never** tell a Client you can get something done when you think you can't.

47.
ENSURE EVERYONE IN YOUR COMPANY UNDERSTANDS THE 'LIFETIME VALUE' OF A CLIENT

A number of years ago, I got some incredibly bad service from a major US airline. **They** had canceled a flight, and because I didn't jump through the hoops exactly right, they were going to charge me for the flight that was cancelled. Now they finally came through and didn't charge me, but if they had held firm, I would have taken away all of our company's business from that airline. I would have told everyone you cannot fly on this airline unless there is no other option.

We do a considerable amount of flying in our business. In fact, I figured in ten years this airline would have lost at least $250,000 if they had held firm to their stupid rule. What is the lifetime value of your Client? Everybody on your team needs to understand the total cost if you treat a Client with indifference, or even worse, rudely, and they leave and never come back again. Make sure everyone on your team understands the lifetime value of a Client, and that you're not just losing the order today, you're likely losing the order and the Client forever.

48.
ENSURE EVERYONE IN YOUR COMPANY KNOWS THAT 'WORD-OF-MOUTH' CAN BE YOUR BEST ADVERTISING OR YOUR WORST ADVERTISING

The cumulative effect of Word-of-Mouth is amazing. Do your people know that, on average, a happy a Client will tell one to three people about your great service?

Do they know that a dissatisfied Client will, on average, tell sixteen people about your poor service?

Always remember word-of-mouth advertising can be your best, or worst, form of advertising.

Remember the story of the airline that almost lost $250,000 worth of our business. I wrote about that in one of my email marketing tips. I didn't print the name of the airline in the article because they eventually made it right. But if they had not made it right, I would have named the airline in this book and in my marketing tip. To date more than 20,000 of these books have been distributed and my email marketing tip goes to more than 25,000 American Retail Supply Clients and who knows how many people they would have told?

Right now, I'm fighting with a yellow pages company that messed up my advertising two years in a row. They printed my 'Bags – Plastic' ad in the 'Store Fixtures' section and my 'Store Fixtures' ad under 'Bags – Plastic.' It makes us look like idiots and they have refused to make it right by crediting my account. If they continue, I may very well warn all my Clients about them.

49.
CHALLENGE INDIVIDUALS TO BE JOHNNY

My favorite Client service book of all time is *The Simple Truths of Service, Inspired by Johnny the Bagger* by Ken Blanchard and Barbara Glanz. I encourage you to get the book and read it. Go to www.AmericanRetailSupply.com and click on Retail Resources, or call 800-426-5708.

Johnny is a nineteen-year old autistic bagger at a grocery store. After watching a Customer service training DVD, Johnny takes it upon himself to put a little extra into his job and provide a little more for each Client. Following Johnny's lead, the attitude of everyone in the store changed in a positive way, the store's sales rose dramatically, and Clients stand in long lines just to be in Johnny's lane. Encourage your people to be Johnny by getting a copy of the book for each team member and then periodically ask, 'How will you be Johnny today?'

50.

TRAIN TEAM MEMBERS TO UNDERSTAND THAT CLIENTS ARE UPSET WITH THE SITUATION

I discussed this a bit in secret #43 – *Train all team members who come in contact with Clients in how to take care of an upset Client*, but this idea is important enough to highlight it again.

When helping upset Clients it's important to work on your self-talk. As Clients are attacking them, many people participate in negative self-talk like, 'I don't have to listen to this kind of stuff.' 'I don't get paid to listen to this.'

The more you say these things to yourself, the more irritated you get and the more you start sounding defensive. Your tone of voice even changes. So instead, while a Client is going at you, practice calming self-talk. You should rehearse your calming talk with something like, 'Hang in there. I can handle this. They'll be finished in a few moments. I can take it. It's not really me.'

In fact in many, maybe even most, cases you did not create the anger. Maybe it's the three bills the Client got in the mail that day or the pressure from his boss. But the Client takes it out on you. Or it may have something to do with your organization and a company policy. Continue to say reassuring things to yourself while maintaining your cool and listening to what the Client is saying.

51.

SERVE THE CLIENT

Post this sign in your lunchroom, by your time clock, in the restroom, in your backroom, in every cubicle... wherever it makes sense for you.

When you see, hear, or meet a Client, all other duties and activities are put on hold. First, foremost, and fanatically... SERVE THE CLIENT!

52.

MAKE SURE EVERYONE UNDERSTANDS THEIR ROLE IN THE SHOW

In secret #31, I discussed Disney training as shown in the *In Search of Excellence* DVD. In that training, Disney says that everyone must understand their role in the show. **Everyone in your organization needs to understand their role in your show,** and their role in your show should be focused on giving Out-Nordstrom Nordstrom Client Service to your Clients.

Everyone at American Retail Supply knows their role in the show is to **Use Your Best Judgment to Take Care of Clients.** That doesn't mean that people just run around making up their own procedures to take care of Clients.

We explain it to our team members this way. Your role in the show is:

#1 Follow the Make-You-Happy Job Requirements
#2 Within the guidelines of the L.E.A.R. (see #43) principle, use your best judgment to take care of Clients and internal customers. (See #15).

So what is a Make-You-Happy Job Requirement? A Make-You-Happy Job Requirement defines exactly how we do each job - that is, each and every thing we do at American Retail Supply. Everything we do has a written procedure. Whether it's greeting a Client, entering an order, stocking shelves, or anything else. Every job has a procedure on how to do it correctly. For many of these job requirements the manager simply wrote up the procedure. For others, a team of people got together and determined the best way to do something. Either way, over time, we've written the proper procedures for doing everything we do.

Here is what is written on the bottom of every Make-You-Happy Job Requirement. It says, 'This Make-You-Happy Job Requirement is designed to ensure we meet or exceed our Client's expectations. Perform exactly like the requirement unless you find it is not in the best interest of your Client. If you find it no longer meets or exceeds our Client's expectations, you are responsible for helping to change it to what we and our Clients and internal customers need.'

Combining this with each team member's 'role in the show' means, if a Make-You-Happy Job Requirement doesn't work to take care of a Client, the team member needs to use his best judgment, to do what he thinks is best to take care of that Client. But their job is not done. Then, the team member who hasn't followed the Make-You-Happy Job Requirement needs to tell their manager that the Job Requirement doesn't work. The manager and the team member are now responsible for revising the requirement.

With this, we all learn what works, what doesn't work, and we continually improve our Client service. In addition, when a new team member joins us, training is very simple because all of their duties have written procedures.

So again, for our team members, their role in the show is to "follow the Make-You-Happy Job Requirement unless it doesn't take care of the Client, and if it doesn't, they use their best judgment to take care of the Client."

You can learn more about Make-You-Happy Job Requirements at www.KLManagementSystem.com.

53.
3 THINGS TO REMEMBER

I'm a firm believer in the K.I.S.S. principle. I first heard of this from a marketing professor at the University of Puget Sound in 1978. The K.I.S.S. principle is:

Keep
It
Simple
Stupid

Our '3 Things to Remember' reinforce our Out-Nordstrom Nordstrom Client Service and yet keep it simple for our team members providing the service. We use these '3 Things to Remember' in many ways. We use them in internal communications, in initial team member training, and in ongoing training.

Our '3 Things to Remember' are:
1. *Do what you do so well that people can't help telling others about you*
2. . . . and then some.
3. What can I do to Make-You-Happy?

The quotation, *'Do what you do so well that people can't help telling others about you'* is from Walt Disney, and it makes a lot of sense! If you, *Do what you do so well that people can't help telling others about you,* ' you'll likely do a good job of making Clients happy.

The second 'Thing to Remember' is . . . **and then some.** What does this mean? When you were a little kid, and your mom said you needed to clean your room before you could go out and play, if you did what you thought mom wanted **and then some,** you probably got to go out and play quickly. If you needed to weed the garden before you got to go play and you weeded it like your dad wanted, **and then some,** you probably got to go play quickly. When you got to school and you did what the teacher asked, **and then some,** you probably did pretty well. If we do **...and then some** with our Clients and internal customers, we'll probably do a darned good job.

The third 'Thing to Remember' is **'What can I do to Make-You-Happy?'** This goes back to the L.E.A.R. principle and our Make-You-Happy Guarantee. This is something we want to reinforce with our new team members, as well as in our ongoing training.

54.
MAKE SURE EVERYONE KNOWS YOUR TABOOS

Do you have any Client service taboos in your business? You should. Taboos are things that are just not tolerated. We have two taboos. The first is:

No - No's

I am the only person who can say <u>NO</u> to a Client. We're dedicated to Out-Nordstrom Nordstrom Client Service. Not just the best Client service in our industry. Not just the best Client service in our area. But the best

Client service – period. So we never want to say no to a Client. But that doesn't mean we have to say yes, at least not right away. See Secret #43.

Our second taboo is:
Nothing less than good Client service is ever acceptable

Our goal is higher than just 'good service,' but we realize that people work at American Retail Supply and people have lots of things going on in their lives. It simply is not realistic that people won't ever have a bad hour or a bad day. **So every American Retail Supply team member knows that slipping to 'good service' is the minimum acceptable. Good service is treating someone with courtesy and respect.**
Sometimes it's not easy to have taboos and enforce them. For example, we had a team member quit in one of our warehouses. Then another one of the warehouse people was rude to a Client. Everyone here knows the rules of Client service at American Retail Supply but we just had someone quit and this warehouse had only three team members. Firing the rude team member was going to make it very hard to get things done. Even though it was going to be hard, the division manager knew what needed to be done; the rude team member was fired.
It wasn't easy. It meant a lot of extra work for the rest of the team, but everyone knew that's what needed to be done. We expect consistent Out-Nordstrom Nordstrom Client Service and we never accept anything less than good Client service. Being rude to a Client is never tolerated, not even once.

55.
USE GOOD TELEPHONE SKILLS - SMILE

Train people in how to answer the phone. Don't assume they know how to answer the phone. After studying a course from The Telephone Doctor, Nancy Friedman (www.telephonedoctor.com), here's how we answer the phone and some of the primary lessons we teach our team:

1. Greeting – Thanks for calling
2. Identify your company – American Retail Supply
3. Tell them what's next – How may I direct your call?

So we get, 'Thanks for calling American Retail Supply, how may I direct your call?'

Yours might be, 'Good morning, Mary's Gift Shop, how may I help you?'

The Telephone Doctor says to use some kind of greeting before saying your business name. Many people are not ready to listen as soon as you pick up the phone, and if you give them the name of your store immediately, they're not ready to hear it. So use a greeting like, 'Thanks for calling' or 'Good Afternoon' before saying your business name. Then give your business name and tell the Client what you want them to do.

Be sure that all of your team members are trained to smile when they're on the phone. In fact, I suggest that you put a mirror next to the phone with the word smile on it. Without question, a smile comes over the telephone. You can get a small acrylic mirror from us here at American Retail Supply.

Teach your team members to have good posture when they're on the phone and to treat that phone call exactly how you would treat a walk-in Client. Give them Out-Nordstrom Nordstrom Client Service.

Be sure that you have a notepad and writing utensils by the phone so you can take care of the Client efficiently and effectively.

56.
CALL PEOPLE BY NAME

The sweetest sounding word to anyone is their name - Use it! One of the best people I know at this is my mentor, friend, and former partner, Dick Thompson. When Dick met somebody, he focused on that person like a laser. You could see it in his eyes. He was going to learn about this person and most certainly learn their name. Dick would ask for their name, and if it wasn't entirely obvious he would ask, 'How do you spell that?" He then was sure to use the person's name in the conversation. When you hear the name, pay attention, learn it, and use it right away in the conversation. Then continue to use it.

When Kerry Thomsen and Paul Marston started managing the Ivar's Seafood Bar in Kent, Washington the store's sales were consistently in the bottom 10% out of the company's 26 stores. Today they rank in the top 10%. They do a lot of things really well and they are incredibly good at **calling customers by name.**

I have lunch at their restaurant often. My guess is that they greet about two out of every three customers by name when they enter the restaurant. Kerry and Paul tell me they each know the names of over 1,000 customers... and they know what most of them order. I'm sure this warm, friendly greeting of calling people by name is one of the reasons their sales have grown to among the best in the chain.

57.
CAPITALIZE CLIENT

Here's another tip I learned from Disney. You likely noticed when I used the word Client or Customer in this book I capitalized it each time. Disney calls their Customer's Guests, and they always capitalize the "G" in Guest. Here at American Retail Supply we call our Customers Clients and we always capitalize Clients. Whether you call your Customers Guests, Customers, Clients, Patients, Members, or Whatever, always capitalize it. Each time you do that it will be one more reminder to you and your team of, "Who's the Boss."

58.
GREET CLIENTS WARMLY WITH A SMILE

I didn't include secret 58 or 59 in the first editions of this book because I didn't want it filled with obvious, no-brainer, information. I have sadly added 'Greet Clients Warmly with a Smile' and 'Say Thank You' because I so seldom get either when I'm out and about.

The sad truth is you need to specifically train your team to greet every Client or prospect with a warm, friendly, sincere, smile.

59.
SAY THANK YOU

Train everyone on your team to thank the Client at the end of every interaction. This includes thanking the Client who doesn't buy.

We train our staff that if you want a prospect to become a Client, treat them like a Client. Like the greeting, this 'thank you' needs to be warm and sincere.

Bonus Secret
All Client Service Problems and Errors are <u>YOUR</u> Errors

President Harry Truman is famous for saying, **"The buck stops here."** It seems we've lost that idea. Whether it's politicians or business leaders, it seems leaders today are more interested in pointing fingers than taking responsibility. Dick Thompson, my mentor, former partner, and the founder of American Retail Supply, taught me long ago when you point your finger at someone else you have three fingers pointing back at you.

When your company delivers less than great Client service you need to understand that it is **your** responsibility to fix it.

Final Thought

Here's one last thing to look for, and how you'll know when your team members truly **get it** and are providing Out-Nordstrom Nordstrom Client Service. You'll know that they "get it" when they start telling you and other team members about the poor Client service they get elsewhere.

Remember, Only Happy Clients Come Back

As I mentioned in the introduction to this book, this book originated as an in-house reference resource for achieving great Customer service in our company, American Retail Supply. I also created the Out-Nordstrom Nordstrom Customer Service System for use in our business to introduce and train new team members in Out-Nordstrom Nordstrom Customer Service and for ongoing Out-Nordstrom Nordstrom Client service. **The Out-Nordstrom Nordstrom Client Service System is now available for your business.** See the last few pages of the book for information on the system.

The Results

Out-Nordstrom Nordstrom Client Service is FUN and getting comments like these from Clients is a big part of that fun.

Mementos Gift Shop, Clark Fork Valley Hospital - Plains, MT - We are a hospital gift shop in rural Western Montana staffed and managed by volunteers. Recently we purchased SmartRegister and after 6 weeks, there is no way we could go back to the "old way." Training for the volunteers with many different computer skill levels was so easy. Our rep from the first days of planning, to opening the shop, to the present, is Mark Turner. He is a <u>treasure!!</u> It doesn't matter what I need, it only takes a call to Mark and he makes it happen. He explained the SmartRegister software and demonstrated it for us at the California Gift Show in July and we started using it full time in the shop. Thanks for everything. The tech support crew for the register is awesome.

Space Needle – Seattle, WA – We like Christy! Sometimes we call for one thing and she reminds us of things we might need, which is good because we don't realize how much stuff we are almost out of sometimes. She also calls to check on us, when she hasn't heard from us for a while!

Northwest Beauty – Spokane, WA – American Retail & Mark Turner are both outstanding in every way. I very much appreciate the very special attention that our company receives from American Retail Supply. Mark deeply cares about the success of our business and helps me to find ways to increase profits & reduce costs too!

Army Surplus – Sandpoint, ID – The system has lived up to its' claims. My business has become easier to manage as well as more profitable. The support that I have received for the retail management program from Mark Turner has been superb. Indeed, he has become a friend in the time we have been doing business. I am always willing to be a reference for your company in the event that you need endorsement for your system and your service.

Hood River Memorial Hospital – Hood River, OR – The Gift Shop really is lovely and we have had so many compliments how elegant it is. The display units really are great and it all fits together very well. Business is booming since we opened, the community has discovered what a nice store it is and all the lovely things we carry. Thanks again for all you did for us, and I hope you're feeling much better and back helping other people with their gift shops!

Kaiser Volunteer Services – Oakland, CA – Your company representative was very helpful. She must have taken ESP101. I had planned on calling in an order but she telephoned first. She also suggested the "teal" plastic bags. I <u>love</u> the color. Thank you for being there!

The Shirt Mine – Breckenridge, CO – I especially like getting the order in by noon for next day delivery.

Security Administration – Puyallup, WA – On extremely short notice, I placed an order for merchandise we were running short on. The sales person said I would receive it the next day and I did. What a relief to have a company follow through on a promise to deliver. What's important is I called on December 22nd during the height of the Christmas rush. The order was delivered on 12/23 midday. Wow, I'm impressed!

Garden City Floral – Missoula, MT – I love Mark! He's been wonderful to work with - helpful and has great suggestions.

Julia's – Portland, OR – I just wanted to let you know that we have been very happy with your company. We can't believe how fast we get our orders (and everything has been there). Thank you, and everyone at American Retail for doing such a great job! Thanks again.

LSG Sky Chefs #1616 – Anchorage, AK – American Retail Supply is excellent at giving my company fast, efficient, friendly service. Sales people have been most helpful in answering questions to insure I am ordering what I want.

Granny's Attic – Vashon, WA – This is the kind of company I want to keep dealing with! When I called to tell you how unhappy we were with the Meto labelers, the sales rep questioned me concerning our needs and we decided on the Dennison labelers. She sent them out immediately, and you are going to give us full credit on the Metos. That's the way I do business and I appreciate your company doing the same. You have a new <u>loyal</u> Customer! Thank you.

Evergreen Club – Spokane, WA – Prompt service appreciated. Ordered one day and received merchandise the next day.

The Octopus' Garden – Richland, WA – I was shipped the wrong size register tape. I called and was told it would be taken care of. The correct tape arrived the <u>next</u> day. Thank you.

Goody's – Bend, OR – We deal with so many companies and have never given so much praise to one company. American Retail Supply does business the way it should be done. Keep up the great work.

Roy's Pharmacy – Tonasket, WA – I like that very seldom do you ever have to wait on the line to talk to someone. My orders arrive very promptly. The sales people are very informed about the product no matter what you may be calling for.

Wight's Home & Garden – Lynnwood, WA – Excellent, fast, courteous service! I order supplies from several companies and whenever I have something to order from American Retail Supply, it's like a nice visit. I usually deal with Janet but other employees have also served me extremely well. Problems that crop up, such as returns, are never problems with your company. Keep up the good work.

Country Cousin – Ketchum, ID – The order came <u>so</u> quickly! Really appreciate the promptness. It made doing my display signs, fixtures & all so much faster.

Oak Glen Christian Conference Center – Yucaipa, CA – You have the <u>best</u> Customer service representatives anywhere! They are always cheerful, helpful and knowledgeable. Keep up the good work.

Buffalo Exchange – Tempe, AZ – Kristen is a gem. I've had many problems with other merchandise suppliers but she has always been helpful, courteous, and efficient. American Retail Supply is now my #1 merchandise supplier. I will always call American Retail first because I know Kristen will assure the quality of service and product availability I need.

Greenhouse Crafts – Glendale Springs, NC – I love talking to the same nice, efficient, helpful salesman year after year. You guys are great.

American Cancer Society, Regional Discovery Shops Manager – Tacoma, WA – I always advise my Discovery Shops to use your company when needing supplies. Your service has always been great.

The Sycamore Tree - Baker City, OR - We purchased the Microsoft Point of Sale System. We absolutely love it. There are a few other stores in town that purchased other products (QuickBooks, etc), and they wish they would have gotten what I did.

Buck Knives – Hauser, ID - Your customer service is phenomenal! You have gone well beyond what one would expect. I cannot really explain how impressed I am. I wish more businesses were half as helpful and responsive as you and American Retail Supply have been.

The Out-Nordstrom Nordstrom Customer Service System

The Out-Nordstrom Nordstrom Customer Service System includes four types of training: Initial Training, New Employee Training, On-Going Training, and Management Team Training. Some of the contents are used in more than one type of training. The initials next to each item in the system refer to the type of training it is used for:

1. **Initial Training, IT** - This is your first training session with your team.
2. **New Employee Training, NE** - This is the training you give to every new hire on their first day of employment.
3. **On-Going Training, OT** - Persistent, consistent ongoing training is critical to your success. Use these tools for on-going customer service training.
4. **Management Team Training, MT** - Training and resources for you and your management team.

Fast Start Guide - IT, MT - Use this step-by-step guide to get Out-Nordstrom Nordstrom Customer Service implemented fast. If you have more than one level of management you'll also use this guide to introduce the system to your management team before you introduce it to your entire team.

In Search of Excellence DVD - IT, NE, OT, MT - Use this special edit of Tom Peters and Robert Waterman's best selling DVD in your Initial Training, New Employee Training, On-Going Training and Management Team Training.

Out-Nordstrom Nordstrom Initial Meeting Customer Service System Training DVD - IT, OT - Use this DVD when you introduce your team to Out-Nordstrom Nordstrom Customer Service and for on-going training.

Initial Training Leader's Guide - IT - Use this Initial Training Leader's Guide for your first time training with your team. You can use the script word-for-word or use it as a guideline when introducing the system to your team.

Initial Training Workbook and Answer Key - IT - Your team members will complete this workbook while they watch the training DVDs. This insures they understand the key points and understand your Out-Nordstrom Nordstrom Customer Service expectations. The answer key is included for you.

Out-Nordstrom Nordstrom New Employee Customer Service System Training DVD - NE - This DVD has the same information as the initial training DVD but it is targeted at new employees. This should be the very first training every new employee receives.

New Employee Training Leader's Guide – NE, MT - Use this guide on the first day of training for each new employee. This training should be led by the new employee's direct supervisor. You can use the Leader's Guide script word-for-word or use it as a guideline when introducing the system to your team.

New Employee Training Workbook and Answer Key - NE, MT - Each new team member will complete this workbook while they watch the training DVDs. This insures that they understand the key points and understand your Out-Nordstrom Nordstrom Customer Service expectations. The answer key is included for you.

Ongoing Training Guidelines – OT, MT - Use these guidelines for your ongoing customer service training.

Ongoing Training #1, Leader's Guide – OT, MT - It's critical that you complete this follow-up training session within the first month of introducing the system to your team. Use this guide to lead your first ongoing training session.

Ongoing Training #2, Leader's Guide – OT, MT - Use this as a guide for your second follow up training session. On-going training sessions from this point forward should be no longer than 20 minutes and can be completed with your entire team or in smaller work groups.

The Book Out-Nordstrom Nordstrom and its Transcription in a MS Word Doc - With your investment in the Out-Nordstrom Nordstrom Customer Service System you have the rights to edit the book *Out-Nordstrom Nordstrom, Creating the World's Best Customer Service,* as you wish to use in your business. You may not want to implement a secret or two in the book, or you may want to add some thoughts of your own, or you may want to expand on certain subjects. You have my permission to alter the book in any way for use in your own business. You only have permission to alter the book for use in your own business. You have no other permission to alter the contents and specifically do not have permission to sell, or otherwise profit from, the altered book, or my book, Out-Nordstrom Nordstrom without prior written agreement from the author, Keith Lee.

Best of Keith Lee's Newsletter Articles - 240 page manual full of articles on Out-Nordstrom Nordstrom-Customer Service.

Best of Marketing Tip of the Week – Seventy-six tips on marketing, customer service, and management. Each tip takes no more than three minutes to read but packs a huge punch to your marketing know-how. Start implementing these ideas and watch your business.

Suitable for Framing – Print these on nice paper and post them throughout your business. Display these in your break room, in cubicles, backroom, offices, and where ever your customers can see them. Yes, let your customers know your customer service expectations. Don't let them be a secret.
  1. Who's the Boss?
  2. Serve the Customer
  3. *Do What You Do So Well That People Can't Help Telling Others About You*
  4. L.E.A.R Guidelines – Make sure everyone in your business has the L.E.A.R. guidelines at their desk, at the cash register or anywhere else your team members may be when they take care of an upset customer.

Resource CD - Most everything listed above is on this CD in MS Word documents so you can tweak it to fit your business' needs as you wish!

Go to

www.ONNCustomerServiceTraining.com
for complete details and pricing for
Out-Nordstrom Nordstrom
Customer Service Training System

Go to page 92 to learn about the **Out-Nordstrom Nordstrom Customer Service System**

For more information go to
ONNCustomerServiceTraining.com
or call
1-855-597-7345